Jane

WITHOUT TARZAN

THE ADVENTURES OF A SINGLE WOMAN

— JANE DODS —

Cover Photography by Richard Romm
Wardrobe by Dolly Marshall

LUMINARE PRESS

WWW.LUMINAREPRESS.COM

Jane without Tarzan
© 2019 Jane Dods

Cover Design: Melissa K. Thomas

Luminare Press
438 Charnelton St., Suite 101
Eugene, OR 97401
www.luminarepress.com

ISBN: 978-1-64388-059-4
LOC: 2018968477

TABLE OF CONTENTS

Prologue

Dateline—Tanzania, Africa, August 3, 1997: I glanced at my watch in the light of my headlamp. It was 4:30 a.m. It was 15-degrees. We had been climbing since 12:30. The summit of Mt. Kilimanjaro was still over four hours away. My body was saying "enough already," but my spirit compelled me to keep climbing—ever seeking a new challenge…

— CHAPTER 1 —

HOLLYWOOD AND THE EARLY YEARS

I ENTERED THE WORLD IN THE HOLLYWOOD HOSPITAL ON December 21, 1935—two weeks early. Even then I was eager to expand my horizons. My dad was a sheep and horse man from New Zealand who arrived in L.A. in 1929. This was just supposed to be a stopover on his way to Argentina to work on the pampas. My mother was born in the (then) outpost of El Paso, Texas, in 1896. She was bi-lingual until age two when the family moved to Oklahoma City—her favorite word being *leche*. Her father was a young canned goods salesman trying to break in his product in this border town. Just after the turn of the century he was promoted to the big town of Oklahoma City where my mother grew up. In 1924, the family relocated permanently to Los Angeles for its drier climate as her father suffered with asthma in the muggy midwest. Meanwhile, before heading down to South America, my dad paid a visit to his brother who had come to Hollywood several years earlier with hopes of breaking into the movies with his (I'm told) fine voice. This did not work out but his fine horsemanship got him plenty of work as an extra in the "oaters" of the day. To make a long story short, my dad never got to the pampas. He met my mother and her family who had become good friends of his brother. Sparks were soon ignited during musical evenings at the family home in the Hollywood Hills (and I'm sure were further ignited in more secluded areas of the neighboring hills). Three years later they were married.

By this time my father was also associated with the movie business. As with his brother, horsemanship turned out to be the key to his employment. His first job was as a stable hand for Darryl Zanuck's polo ponies (Zanuck being the head honcho of 20th Century-Fox Studios). Polo loomed large in Southern California in the 30s, with regular matches held at the Will Rogers Polo Grounds in the Pacific Palisades, adjacent to Santa Monica. Before long, my dad graduated to being a member of Zanuck's team. I never saw him play, but my brother, who was three years older, vaguely remembers going to a match. Not long afterwards, Zanuck took my dad under his wing and brought him into his studio grooming him to become head of the film editing department. My dad's "qualifications" for this job were that he cut a fine figure and had a classy "British" accent—great for studio PR! An important part of this job was accompanying films to be premiered in out-of-town locales. He frequently flew to New York, and in 1939 he and Tyrone Power (a top star of the era) traveled together to Mexico City for the premiere of *Blood and Sand* (a major bullfighting epic of the day). They were treated royally, even hobnobbing with the president of Mexico and his entourage.

In 1937, when I was two, we moved to a lovely home in the Cheviot Hills section of Los Angeles (right down the road from 20th Century-Fox Studios on Pico Boulevard). What a carefree childhoood I enjoyed—dad gainfully employed in this "depression" era and mom home to cater to my brother's and my every need. The movie business was booming because it offered cheap entertainment for folks with little income. Admission at that time was no more than a quarter. As children, we didn't realize how lucky we were. We needed no key to the front door and used the neighborhood as our own private playground—climbing trees, jumping over fences into our neighbors' yards when playing hide-and-seek, or dodging cars while playing kick-the-can in the street.

My only sore point (and it was a major one) was my mother's over-protectiveness. I didn't come along until she was almost 40, and having had a son she was thrilled to now have a daughter to "cuddle and curl." The cuddle part was fine, the curls not so much (in fact, one of my major disappointments as a child was not being able to get a crew cut in the summer like my brother Bill). And I would much rather tag along with Bill and his friends than engage in paper dolls and tea parties. Needless to say, mom loved to dress me up in frilly little frocks when I would have much preferred my brother's jeans and T-shirts. Lastly, she was very fearful of my "getting hurt" in rough activities. I'm sure this attitude only spurred my determination to become even more adventuresome.

I was very fortunate to have a true "best friend," Ann, (a BFF in today's lingo), from kindergarten to junior high school. Her dad also worked in the movie business, as a cameraman. We lived just two blocks apart and were practically inseparable. In those days there was no technology to interfere with our creativity and fun. Radio and 78 records were the media of the day. One of our activities was the "string game" where we would tie string in the bushes to make various patterns (don't ask me where we came up with that!). A big benefit of going to Ann's was that her father had put up a tether ball pole in the vacant lot next to their home (never mind that it wasn't on their property!). And never mind that Ann was taller than I was and usually wound up whipping the ball around the pole above my head—it was still great fun. Jacks were also good for coordination and could keep us amused for hours, as could Canasta. The vacant lot next door became a wonderful playground in the spring when the grass grew tall. We'd tromp through creating paths and build forts or whatever. Those were golden years.

My well-ordered childhood, however, did not blind me to the outside world. I knew my dad came from a far-away place, and I always had a curiosity about what was beyond my back yard. I loved maps and learning where different countries were. In 6th grade our class painted a mural of the Amazon jungle while studying South America. This was, for me, the highlight of the term. It was around that time I began reading the "boys" series of adventure stories by

Howard Pease. The main character, Todd Moran, was a teenage boy who traveled the world on a tramp steamer, and I yearned to do the same. Little did I know at that time what adventures lay in store.

One other thing I should mention about growing up in the '40s was the effect of WWII. In school we purchased savings stamps which were later converted into war bonds—$18.75 in stamps got you a $25.00 bond. We also dutifully planted "victory gardens" (ours was in a vacant lot across the street—not our property either!). Then there were the ration stamps limiting certain purchases—particularly gas. I think we had a "B" sticker—indicating moderate need. My dad's contribution to the war effort was being an air raid block warden. Whenever the sirens went off he had to go out in our neighborhood and make sure our neighbors had their blackout curtains in place. Lastly, had I been a bit older I would probably have joined the Waves—they got to wear such great-looking uniforms and go out on ships (or so I thought at the time)!

Of course, upon reaching my teens I couldn't wait to drive and got my license at 16. To top that off my dad bought me a car—a '41 Chevy coupe—for $400. I was awed at the amount of money he spent on me. Needless to say, I was quite popular as the only girl to drive to high school. My friends and I had great fun tooling around town. Spending weekends on the beach at Santa Monica was a favorite activity as was going to the Hollywood Bowl on summer nights. We would park in the construction zone for the Hollywood Freeway and then walk across Highland Avenue to the Bowl and our 50-cent seats (I think they still offer those seats for $1.00). For a couple of seasons, a friend and I ushered here in order to get free admission. We got to wear snappy blue satin capes adorned with the Hollywood Bowl logo.

— CHAPTER 2 —

"COMING OUT" IN THE 50s

After graduating from high school in 1954, I attended U.C.L.A. (Go Bruins!) for two years as a music major. I didn't have any particular career goals and I liked music, so why not? It was also very cheap. I think registration was about $75.00 a term, with books being the only additional expense. Also, I lived at home, so housing was not an issue. It was at this time that I recognized my sexuality and "came out" as gay. I knew very clearly that boys, dating same, and marriage were not for me. There were no ifs, ands, or buts about it. Not only was I gay, I was also very independent. I couldn't wait to strike out on my own. The clandestine aspect of being gay in the '50s also appealed to me. I enjoyed being part of a "secret society." Books with titles such as "The Love That Dare Not Speak Its Name" were read avidly behind closed doors. It was exciting to me to be a part of this culture. I can't say it was this positive for everyone (there was definitely some harassment going on at the time), but for me it worked—even if I didn't shout it out to the world. Of course there were literally no gay resources in the city at the time. There were, however, a handful of gay bars which one heard about through the grapevine. The first one I went to was called the If Club in a less than upscale part of the city. A friend and I drove downtown in my little Chevy and walked boldly through the front door with our U.C.L.A. reg cards in hand for ID. Those cards did not indicate age (we were only 19) so we were not allowed to drink, but I think the door person took pity on us "little lezzies" and let us in to soak up the atmosphere over Cokes. There was another gay bar across the street on Western called the "Open Door" which we visited from time to time in later years. Another watering hole, less frequently visited, was Georgia Lee's. We didn't go here often since it was a fair distance east of L.A. off one of the budding freeways. This establishment required a membership. Georgia interviewed you, and if you passed muster you got a "party pass." Since bars were the only social places for gays to hang out at that time, and I was under age, I didn't do very much of it. Fortunately, I later met a gay guy at Douglas Aircraft where I got a job after my two years at U.C.L.A. He had a partner, and we had tons of fun together. We all lived near Santa Monica and spent most weekends on the sand and at the bars at the "gay beach" in Venice—adjacent to "Muscle Beach" (which my male friends very much enjoyed). Baby oil, with a little iodine dropped in for color, was the "sun tan lotion" of choice, and we slathered it on in hopes of a gorgeous tan (what's SPF?) Being blue-eyed and fair haired, this never quite worked for me. I do, however, remember some memorable sunburns. Also around this time we would often spend a Saturday or Sunday at a place called The Canyon Club—a private gay club in Los Angeles' Topanga Canyon (I still have my membership card). This was a sprawling resort-type place in the Santa Monica Mountains between the Pacific Ocean and the San Fernando Valley. We would drive up from the coast on Highway 101, usually in the early afternoon, hang out by the pool (and bar) and later head inside for dinner and dancing (slow dancing, mmm!) The owner was an ex-cop who would alert us by flashing a blue light if we were about to be visited by the law. At that point we simply changed partners for their inspection and regrouped after the fuzz left (perhaps it was a city law that such "dens of iniquity" needed to monitored). Looking back, I'm amazed that we made it home (mostly) safely after driving down through that curvy canyon often in the dark, after our imbibing. We must have had some gay angels on our side! I did have one incident when a car coming from the other direction drove me off the side of the road, but there were no significant injuries (except for the cars).

— CHAPTER 3 —

U.C.L.A., FIRST APARTMENT, ROUTE 66

As previously mentioned, I graduated from high school in 1954 and enrolled at U.C.L.A. Not having any specific career goals, however, I left after two years but wouldn't have missed this collegiate experience for anything. The Bruins won the Rose Bowl the first year I was there. What a thrill it was to march proudly down Westwood Boulevard in a victory celebration sporting our rooters' caps and making lots of noise. Another favorite memory was performing card stunts during half-times at football games. The students were given a stack of colored cards (about 12" x 12") and would hold one of them up at a time, at the direction of a leader, to form a scene of some kind or perhaps just a word of two (i.e., Go Bruins). Although we couldn't see the results of our own efforts, we could watch the other teams' stunts across the field. In this age of flashy, high-tech, ear-blasting entertainment, I look back on these simple homemade efforts with great fondness.

I now had an apartment in Venice Beach—four blocks from the ocean—and an office job at Douglas Aircraft. During WWII these aircraft factories were camouflaged with make-believe villages on top. My rent was $54 a month which was easily affordable on my secretarial salary of approximately the same amount each week. I decided office work was the best fit for me since I could quit whenever I got the urge to travel and easily get another job when I returned home. I loved the Venice area—hanging out on the beach on weekends and frequenting the nearby coffee houses on many an evening, This was the "beatnik" era, and although I wasn't a real beatnik I thoroughly enjoyed mixing with the alternative types (and still do).

In 1958 I undertook my first long-distance travel adventure. Having experienced the coffee houses in Venice, I got wind of Greenwich Village and its denizens (not to mention the gay life which I heard was flourishing there) and decided I must have a look. So I hopped in my '57 Ford Fairlane (a real beauty!) and headed east. This would be my first experience at "car camping." Being only 5'2", stretching out on my car's bench seat at night was quite comfortable. Gas stations provided my hygiene needs. At that time, gas was running about 22 cents a gallon. I even hit a gas war in Texas where it was only 18.9 cents! I traveled the old Route 66—from L.A. to Chicago—and then went on to New York. I LOVED being on the road on my own. I wasn't as wild as Jack Kerouac, but I think we both had the same spirit. When I reached Chicago I spent a couple of days exploring some of the famous sights I had heard about (Marshall Field's, the Loop, the "el" etc.). Then a brief sojourn through Canada before heading south to Manhattan. I easily made my way to Greenwich Village and in a couple of days found a room on West 11th Street (between 5th and 6th). The room was very small with bath and kitchen down the hall, but it was only $11 a week and had a window overlooking the street with a beautiful tree right outside. After getting settled (which didn't take long), I immediately signed up with a temp office agency and was soon sent out on various assignments in Manhattan. In my spare time I explored all that the Big Apple had to offer—from the coffee houses (which came up to my expectations) to Central Park to Broadway to Cherry Grove on Fire Island and all the intrigue the gay bars had to offer. It was all a fantastic experience. I even managed to see "West Side Story in its second year of production. Musical comedy is probably my favorite musical genre. My parents introduced me to "Oklahoma" in 1943, so seeing a Broadway hit on Broadway was like magic. After soaking all of this up for three months, I headed back west. A friend had sublet my apartment while I was gone.

— CHAPTER 4 —

VIVE LA FRANCE

IN THE EARLY 60s, I WAS SHARING A HOUSE WITH TWO OTHER girls in Benedict Canyon—a scenic woodsy canyon between Hollywood and the San Fernando Valley (later in the decade it would become the infamous site of the grisly Tate-La Bianca murders). I landed a job with a PR firm in Beverly Hills which handled the accounts of several movie stars (including Roz Russell). As a statistical typist I got to type up some very interesting balance sheets! Life went along quite pleasantly until one evening I went to the movies and saw "Paris Blues" with Paul Newman.

That was it. I didn't fall in love with Paul Newman, but I did fall in love with Paris. In December of 1961 I sold my lovely Ford, purchased a one-way plane ticket and headed to the City of Lights. When I arrived, my first job was to secure housing. I headed directly from the airport to the Latin Quarter, which I had heard so much about. After several nights in a hotel there I found an apartment. I had hoped to reside in this interesting part of town, but could not find anything in my price range. Instead, I wound up in the Pigalle area of Montmartre (just steps from the Moulin Rouge). It was a 7-story walk-up with no elevator. If you wanted light on the stairs you pushed a button at each landing. My apartment had two rooms on the top floor which had originally been maids' quarters. The bath was a washtub in the kitchen, and the toilet was of the "squat" variety outside my front door and off the hallway. Despite the lack of amenities, I couldn't have asked for lodgings with a better view. I literally overlooked th rooftops of Paris! And the magnificent cathedral, Sacre Coeur, rose up just behind me. The apartment did not come with a refrigerator so I had to shop almost daily for perishables (putting them on a windowsill overnight). This was not a problem since there was a wonderful market street, Rue des Martyrs, just steps from my building. Here I could buy everything I needed, including horsemeat, which I tried but didn't care for. A golden horsehead identified these butcher shops. I became a true Parisian shopper with my baguette tucked under one arm and my string bag of groceries clutched in the other. The beverage of choice was definitely wine. Ah, yes, *vin rouge ordinaire*. It was pretty ordinary, all right, but at the equivalent of about 25 cents a liter, who's complaining!

My second job was to find a job. Ever the optimist, I figured I could land work with one of the American firms in town (after all, I was a super secretary). There was only one small problem, the extent of my French was pretty much limited to *bon jour* and *merci*. In my naivete, I hadn't realized that foreign workers should have at least a minimal knowledge of the language of the country in which they seek employment. Consequently, I enrolled in *L'Aliance Francais* (a French language school) to help me in this endeavor. While there I met two German girls who were working as *au pairs* (nannies/housekeepers). Although I was not at all fond of either children or housework, I needed a job. And if I was going to be able to stay in Paris I'd better get one soon. I began reading the classified ads in the English-language, European Edition of the New York Herald Tribune. Indeed, there were a number of listings, but they all sounded rather awful. One even had me sleeping in a bunk bed in the same room with the kids! Before long I reached a nice-sounding American man who asked about my qualifications. I admitted that I had never worked in the nanny field but was willing to do whatever was required. Mr. Murphy asked what my line of work was, and when I told him it was secretarial he said to come and see him. It turned out that he was the European representative of Massachusetts Mutual Life Insurance which dealt solely with American military and diplomatic personnel. His secretary was a Swiss girl whose English was not up to par for the job. So instead of becoming the nanny, I became his secretary (being fluent in English). The office was in his lovely apartment in the fashionable 16th *arrondissement* (where he lived with his wife and two children)—a short Metro ride from my newly-acquired apartment. Although I was overjoyed to get the job it wasn't all roses. Mr. Murphy could be an overbearing jerk at times and bring me close to tears with his criticism. He was Irish and a retired military man from West Point. Need I say more? His way of apologizing for his poor behavior was to leave a carton of Salems for me to find in my desk drawer the next morning (he had PX privileges at the military bases where he sold insurance). Yes, in those days I was a smoker. American cigarettes were 60 cents a pack which I could not afford, so I smoked smelly, non-filtered *Galoises* for only about 25 cents a pack. It was almost worth it to get yelled at from time to time to get my Salems! And then there were the outbursts between Mr. Murphy and his young Costa Rican wife, Maria. She was a fiery Latina, and they sometimes got into some major bi-lingual shouting matches. Mrs. Murphy and I got along fine, however. She was just my age, 26, (Mr. M was 42). When hubby left town to peddle his wares at various European military bases and embassies we would often go out to lunch and have a lovely time together. All in all, my work must have been satisfactory, as Mr. Murphy kept me on the job for 16 months.

During that summer, two of my very good friends from L.A. came over for a month-long visit (traditionally, Europeans take their vacations during the month of August, and since I was a temporary European, so did I). They had arranged to pick up a Citroen Deux Chaveaux (a tin can on wheels, but actually quite reliable) at a dealership just outside of Paris. They told me it was a "white knuckler" driving into the city, but they made it unscathed. The full price of the car was about $700, and it was to be shipped back to the States after our trip. Two of the car's unique features were the windshield wipers which had to be activated by hand

and the gas gauge which was a dipstick (also activated by hand!). We drove this amazing little vehicle to the French Riviera (which even back then had its complement of topless sunbathers), down through the Italian Riviera to Rome and Venice and then back over the Brenner Pass through Austria and Germany before returning to Paris. Unfortunately, we missed Florence. We had noted a sign on the way to Rome pointing to Firenze, but since none of us had ever heard of it we kept on driving! We mostly stayed at youth hostels for about $1.50 a night and were just about able to keep to the "Europe of $5.00 a Day" budget. At month's end, my friends were having such a good time they were not ready to return. One of them stayed for another month, and the other one for nearly four months (I don't think my landlady was ever the wiser). It was great to have the company, and we had a lot of adventures in my spare time. Unfortunately, the Citroen didn't make it back to the U.S. One evening as I was driving through the Bois du Boulogne I had an unexpected run-in with a French driver, and the car received mortal wounds. Happily, there were no human injuries.

I had wanted to leave Paris after twelve months, but Mr. Murphy had not found a replacement secretary by that time and bribed me with some extra francs to stay on until he did. I eventually left France in April, 1963, sailing on the Queen Elizabeth I from Le Havre to New York. Although my accommodations were below deck (which I shared with three other women), during the day I had the same view as the first-class passengers. How lovely to be snuggled up cozily in a woolen blanket in my deck chair gazing out at the sea. The QE I was a passenger ship, not a cruise ship—no silly games, no shopping malls, no midnight buffets (at least not in my class). The enjoyment was the journey itself. When we sailed into New York and passed the Statue of Liberty I felt like an immigrant, with tears close at hand. Sixteen months was a long time to be away, and I was thrilled to be home again. The first thing I did after checking into a local "Y" was to buy a jar of peanut butter and a loaf of squishy white bread to spread it on. As good as the bread was in Europe I missed some of the familiar U.S. comestibles from time to time. A minor tragedy occurred during my Paris stay when I splurged a good many francs on a bottle of American ketchup at a "foreign" food store, only to have the paper sack break in a Metro station on my way home. I never did manage to have ketchup in my Parisian kitchen cupboard. Actually, the *frites* were quite tasty on their own.

When I arrived in New York I was practically broke, but not to worry. Mr. Murphy (bless his heart!) had arranged for me to work in the New York office of Mass Mutual for about a month so as to earn money enough to get me back to L.A. I then found a "Drive-Away" service where people drove other people's cars to various destinations in the country and was soon on my way west, not in a snappy Ford Falcon, but in a sporty red Chevy. It felt great to be "on the road" again. My association with Mass Mutual didn't end in New York. When I arrived back in L.A. they, unexpectedly, offered me a job in the local office. That turned out to be quite memorable, as it was in that office that I first got the news of JFK's assasination.

After several years I moved on to a job as secretary to the Director of the U.C.L.A. Art Galleries, Dr. Frederick Wight. Dr. Wight was a devotee of modern art, something about which I knew very little. He was writing a book on the subject and would dictate to me at the typewriter. This was better than any class I could have taken on the subject. Just outside my window was the university's beautiful sculpture garden with examples of some of the art I was learning about. These gardens also made a great lunch spot. As much as I enjoyed this segment of my life my feet began to get itchy again several years later.

— CHAPTER 5 —

HEADING DOWN UNDER
Australia and New Zealand

IN 1969 I BOARDED ANOTHER SHIP, THE *S.S. CANBERRA* (OF the British P & O Lines), for a two-and-a-half week voyage from L.A. to Sydney, Australia with $600 in my pocket to last me a year. No worries. I planned to get work when I arrived Down Under. At least I (mostly) spoke the language of the country I was visiting this time!

I always knew I would get to this part of the world someday and visit my relatives in New Zealand. I didn't want to spend an entire year in that tiny country, however, so I headed first to Sydney. What a wonderful, sprawling, vibrant city! Its setting on the harbor is magnificent, overlooking the iconic Sydney Harbour Bridge and the Opera House with its architectural "sails." When I arrived, the opera house had just been completed but was not yet open to the public. I found myself a swell two-room flat in the Kings Cross section of the city and set up housekeeping. In short order I was working for Drake Personnel (the Aussie equivalent of Kelly Girls). As I said, I spoke English, but I did have to adjust to some non-Americanisms such as "cheque" for "check" and "footpath" for "sidewalk," among others. One of my most memorable assignments was working at a distillery. We sat on whiskey barrels while doing the paperwork to process the spirits and we were allowed a nip at break time if we were so inclined! My visa did not officially allow me to work abroad, but at this time Australia was in need of various types of workers and my American accent was not questioned. With this work I was able to fully support myself while still hanging on to most of my original $600.

After several months I met a couple of girls who were going to pick apples in Tasmania. At that point I wasn't even sure where Tasmania was, but I soon learned that it was Australia's island state—some 150 miles south of the continent. Its moniker is the "Apple Island." Fruit-picking sounded fun to me, so I traded in my typewriter for a ladder and a leather pouch. It was early March and just about harvest time (Fall, Down Under). The girls I had spoken with said I shouldn't have any trouble finding a job, and I didn't. I boarded a boat from Melbourne heading south and some eight hours later landed in Devonport, on Tasmania's north coast. In a couple of days I hooked up with an orchard (no experience necessary). The work would not begin for about ten days, so in the meantime I backpacked a beautiful 50-mile trail in Cradle Mountain-Lake St, Clair National Park. I bought a cheap canvas rucksack and sleeping bag, threw in some food and a few personal items and was off. No tent was necessary as there were huts approximately ten miles apart. The huts were basic, consisting of a number of sleeping platforms and a fireplace. Sometimes "mattresses" were left by prior occupants—assorted piles of flora. Any cooking was done over a fire in the fireplace (wood provided and expected to be replenished before leaving). The trek was fairly strenuous but worth every step of the way—from stunning alpine scenery to glacial lakes to rainforests where my bath of the day was sometimes a mud bath. Many wallabies (small kangaroos) call this area home, and it was delightful to cross paths with them now and then. I ended up at Lake St. Clair, Australia's deepest lake. This was my first experience backpacking, and I loved it!

After divesting myself of the muck of the trail I hitchhiked back to Devonport to begin work. I had no qualms about hitchhiking (although I wouldn't have done it in the U.S.). I found lodging with a family in a private home—two rooms and a private bath to call my own. Mom, dad and seven children lived in the rest of the house.

What a find! Room AND board for $10 a week, and all the veggies were straight out of the backyard garden. Another perk was that the wife packed my lunch every day to take to the orchard (along with a thermos of tea). One morning I thanked her for fixing my lunch and she replied, "Why, what was wrong with it!" A taste for Vegemite was bound to develop—although not overwhelmingly! The work itself was pretty easy. We not only picked apples, but pears as well (my friends back in L.A. referred to me as the "Pear Princess" when I returned home). Most of the time we were perched on ladders, reaching out to pluck the fruit and deposit it into the pouches we wore over our shoulders and which hung down in front. When the pouch was full we climbed down, emptied it into a bin, and returned to our trees.

We worked an 8-hour day with lunch and two tea breaks. The pay was 82 cents an hour which was ample to cover my modest needs in Devonport. I bought a bicycle for $15 to get me around on my time off. One day, after working for about a month I got a real scare. I was up on my ladder picking away when two official-looking black cars drove into the orchard. Oh dear—they had found out I was working illegally! But no, they were from the local newspaper and wanted to do a story about the Yank working in Tasmania. Of course, I practically bought out the edition, which included a front-page photo, to send copies of the article to friends back in America!

When the season ended, after three months, I found myself once more on the Australian mainland. Now it was time to explore some of the more far-reaching parts of the vast continent. I signed up for a 3-week bus-camping adventure. We traveled by bus during the day, setting up small canvas tents at night wherever we wound up. Leaving Sydney, we headed northwest up the Gold Coast through Brisbane. A bit further north we turned inland into the bush, covering miles and miles of undeveloped land. From time to time we would come across aboriginal settlements. My favorite souvenir is a wooden carving of a crocodile which I watched being made by one of the residents. A group of nearly-naked ashy-black men sat around a fire putting finishing touches on their carvings with the use of heated wire coat hangers (which they surely didn't use to hang up their clothes!). Eventually we reached Darwin in the tropical north. We had a look at the very large WWII cemetery there and later took a river boat ride which we shared with crocodiles, but Crocodile Dundee was nowhere to be seen!

Then it was due south through the red heart of the country—an unbelievably vast area of (mostly) uninhabited land. The road was not paved for the most part but was very well-graded which made for a remarkably smooth ride. The red dust, however, got into everything! When we stopped for the night all our goods had to be shaken out. After some days we reached Alice Springs, take-off point for Ayers Rock (the world's largest monolith) some 250 miles southwest. Cultural sensitivity was not what it is today, so I climbed this amazing hunk of rock in the middle of the desert (climbing today is still allowed, but discouraged out of respect for aboriginal beliefs). Chains were bolted in various places on the way to the top to help climbers maintain their footing on the steep, slippery surface. Once back on the ground, I circumnavigated the monolith on foot and marveled at the many artifacts still visible from ancient times.

The next bump in the road was Coober Pedy, otherwise known as the Opal Capital of the World. More than half the folks who live here (some 3,500 at present) make their homes underground to escape the intense summer heat (often knocking 125-degrees). We took a tour of one of these homes, and although it had all the necessary amenities, I would not want to live below ground. The payoff for many (finding opals), however appears to be worth it. I bought a stone which I later had mounted on my New Zealand grandmother's wedding ring. A few days later found us in Adelaide on the south Australian coast, and from there we headed east back to Sydney. I felt I had gotten a wonderful look at this amazing continent, except for Western Australia. Some 40 years later I flew back to Sydney and boarded the Indian-Pacific Railroad to Perth to complete my Aussie odyssey.

My final two weeks in this part of the world were spent in New Zealand visiting relatives and doing some sightseeing. I headed first to Gisborne, situated on Poverty Bay on the country's east coast. This is where my dad first opened his eyes in 1900. In 2000, one hundred years later, I returned to N.Z. to run the Millennium Marathon. More on this later. On my first visit, however, there was no running—just getting acquainted. My relatives treated me like visiting royalty. It was great to finally get to meet some of them. What they assumed, incorrectly, however, was that I was an accomplished horsewoman—NOT! When my dad made the decision to stay in L.A. he became a total city boy. His children got no instruction in horsemanship. We got introduced to pony rides in the park or a whirl on the local merry-go-round (including a wonderful one on the Santa Monica Pier). So, when my relatives took me on a 3-hour ride I could barely sit down for dinner that evening. Fortunately there were no more rides, just a lot of motoring through this little jewel of a country. Everything looked so neat and well-cared for. People seemed to take great pride in their homes. I noticed little or no shabbiness. And the friendliness I encountered was second to none. I visited only the North Island on this trip—the home of marvelous geothermal activity. Rotorua is a "hot bed" of gurgling mud, hissing steams and geysers. It was fascinating to walk around this area and behold nature's wonders. My farewell dinner in New Zealand was a delicious leg of lamb (what else). It is said that there are more sheep than people in N.Z. What a tasty and memorable way to leave my father's homeland surrounded at the table by my kiwi family. I LOVE being half a kiwi! It was at that dinner that I was presented with my grandmother's wedding ring.

— CHAPTER 6 —

ALOHA OI

I HAD HOPED TO FINISH UP MY SOUTH SEAS ADVENTURE BY working on Australia's Great Barrier Reef at one of the tourist hotels, but by the time I finished visiting relatives in New Zealand all the seasonal jobs were filled. I was not quite ready to return home, so stopped in Hawaii on the way back. Here I found a studio apartment in Waikiki, bought a motor scooter, and signed up with Kelly Girls. I scooted around town to assignments during the week and played on the beach on weekends. I also joined the local hiking club. We most always returned from our treks covered in mud due to the island's lush, wet environment. In time, I met a like-minded gay woman who was attending the University of Hawaii, and we had some excellent adventures. I remained in Hawaii for about four months—until the rains started in November—then flew back to L.A., completing my South Seas sojourn.

Ten years later (1980), after having begun my running "career," I returned to Hawaii to run the Honolulu Marathon. That year the race fell on December 7. Standing in front of the Aloha Tower in the pre-dawn darkness certainly gave one pause to remember that fateful date in 1941. In 1985 I was once again back in Hawaii to run The Great Hawaiian Foot Race. This was a mega-event put on by Dr. Jack Scaff (a local running guru). We ran approximately 17 miles a day for two weeks, circling both the islands of Oahu and Maui. It was not a competitive race except for a small group of elite runners. We could take as much time as we needed, winding up at a campground each night where a catered dinner was brought in. The next morning we were sent off after a delicious catered breakfast. A great feeling of camaraderie developed within the group, and we were sorry to see the "race" come to an end. Olympian Kenny Moore was one of the elite runners. He and I both now live in Eugene.

Jane Dods

— CHAPTER 7 —

THE RECORDING INDUSTRY

When I returned to L.A. from down under in 1970 I was 35 and told myself it was probably time to find a "real job" (with benefits, etc.). I headed back to the temp agencies hoping to be sent somewhere I would like to work permanently. As luck would have it, in a few months' time I was given an assignment at ABC Records—the recording arm of the American Broadcasting Company. I began as a temp secretary, and it was a good fit. After a couple of months I was offered a permanent position with the company and in time was promoted to assistant secretary to the Director of A & R (Artists and Repertoire). This guy was the personal liaison to the label's artists and guided them through their association with the company. I did the paperwork. Some of our artists were Steely Dan, Jim Croce, Three Dog Night, and Dusty Springfield. I remember one afternoon when my boss called me into his office where he was meeting with Ms. Springfield and asked me to get her a cup of tea. I was about to leave the office when she called out, "Just a minute," and pulled out a tea bag from her bra (obviously her favorite brand!). Often lavish parties were held to celebrate an artist's new release, and it was fun to mingle with the celebs. Much to my disappointment, about five years later the company was taken over by MCA Records, and I was not invited to join the crew in Universal City, so back to the temp scene once again. This was not altogether bad, however, as I was again able to hit the road with more frequency.

— CHAPTER 8 —

AROUND THE WORLD
IN 40 DAYS

NOT LONG AFTER MY RELEASE FROM ABC RECORDS IN THE late 70s, I decided to take advantage of my newly-acquired free time and take a jaunt around the world. Happily, my good friend Art was of like mind and we started making plans. One of the places we particularly wanted to visit was the (then) USSR. A mutual friend of ours was of Lithuanian heritage and we wanted, among other things, to visit her homeland and report back. All travel to the USSR at that time had to go through the national Soviet travel agency, Intourist. There was absolutely no private booking. We also found that there was no Intourist office in the U.S., so faxes and telephone calls were needed to cross the pond to the Intourist office in London. Our plan was to fly from L.A. to London and then travel overland for the rest of the journey until our flight home from Japan. This worked out very well. After the flight to London, we would take the boat-train to Paris (before the Chunnel) and then continue by train to Berlin, Warsaw, the Baltic states of Lithuania, Latvia, and Estonia and then into the USSR through St. Petersburg and Moscow. There we would board the Trans-Siberian Railway to Vladivostok in the Soviet Far East where we would pick up a Japanese ship to Tokyo. And finally, from Tokyo, we would fly Philippine Airlines (via Manilla) back to L.A. Our plans worked out very well—Intourist being most efficient (as they darn well better be!). After a couple of days (and a couple of plays) in London we headed to Paris. Here we enjoyed another few days revisiting sites each of us had enjoyed on previous trips (including my old neighborhood of the 60s). My venerable old apartment building looked just as it did nearly 20 years earlier, although I couldn't quite say quite the same for myself. Never mind! Next stop Berlin. During our exploration of the then divided city we noted that the subway did not stop at a number of stations which traveled though the Eastern sector. One could visit the East, however, but only by private tour buses through Checkpoint Charlie. After careful scrutiny of the passengers and the bus itself, we were driven through the checkpoint and taken on a closely guided (and guarded) tour. The city of East Berlin definitely had a rather somber feel about it as opposed to the more vibrant West. Before the return trip the bus driver carefully checked the underside of our bus with a mirror to make sure there were no hangers-on (literally). Seeing the wall as we drove through the city was very sobering.

From Berlin we made our way to Warsaw. This city was pretty much destroyed during WWII, but the people did a magnificent job of rebuilding it—visitors would have a hard time realizing the buildings weren't original—the old-world charm had definitely been replicated. Our stay here was quite inexpensive as the black market was rampant. Normally, we wouldn't use this "currency exchange," but it was offered so openly we felt it was safe (and as it turned out, it was). Dinners for a dollar or two were great as were cheap sleeps. An event I will always remember is seeing the word "Solidarnosk" scrawled on the sidewalk. This is an image I had seen published in the L.A. Times which was closely following the labor troubles in Poland at the time. This word literally meant solidarity and was the name of the first trade union in Warsaw not controlled by the communist party. It was championed by labor activist Lech Walesa who later became president of Poland and for whom the airport in Gdansk was later named. I think this image struck me because it was the first time I had felt up close and personal with a major international event.

While on the platform awaiting the train to Lithuania, Art and I became international smugglers. A guy came up to Art and made a request—Would he please take a pair of jeans to a friend of his in Vilnius, the capital of Lithuania and our destination? We agreed, and Art put this contraband in his suitcase where no one would suspect the pants weren't his if our bags were checked—they weren't. When we got off the train, a guy motioned to us and we "delivered the goods" without incident. Shortly afterwards we found our Intourist guide in the station, as planned. During our time in the Soviet Union we were always met at the train station by Intourist personnel and driven to our hotel. From there, as far as we knew, we were free to do as we liked. We had made plans for our daily itineraries before we left the States. We would sometimes be silly in our room and ask if anyone was listening to us (we couldn't spot any microphones). Before leaving Lithuania I bought a decorative little container and filled it with native soil to give to my good friend Stella. We then traveled north through the two other Baltic States—Latvia and Estonia. In Estonia, I picked up a keepsake for my Estonian ex-boss at MCA, Ulo. He had fled the USSR just prior to WWII and immigrated to New York (I wonder how easy that would be in 2019).

Leaving the Baltic states, we headed east towards Leningrad (now St. Petersburg). It is Russia's second largest city—sometimes called the Northern Venice. And what a beautiful city it is, situated on the banks of the magnificent Volga River. We spent several days here—much of it strolling along the river and taking in the fascinating waterfront sights. And, of course, no visit to this city would be complete without a visit to the Winter Palace. From 1732 to 1917 this was the residence of Russian monarchs. Today, the restored palace houses the Hermitage Museum—the second largest museum in the world. It was founded in 1764 by Catherine the Great and has been open to the public since 1862. Neither my friend Art nor I were particular "museum people" but we couldn't help but be impressed by the art treasures of the ages displayed here.

Leaving Leningrad, we hopped down to Moscow—some 400 miles to the south. When the train pulled into Leningradsky Station (one of 9 railway stations in the city) it was hard to believe we were actually in this famous historic city "behind the iron curtain." Of course our Intourist pals were there to greet us and drive us to our hotel—a rather plain edifice—but with enough amenities to keep us comfortable, i.e. clean beds and running water. In the Soviet Union all large hotels have what Art and I called the "floor matron" on each floor—usually a lady of some size planted behind a desk which overlooked her domain. Whenever we left our room we had to hand over the key to be retrieved upon our return. Probably my most impressionable sight in Moscow was St. Basil's Cathedral with its fairytale-like turrets rising up out of Red Square. It was constructed in the mid-16th century by order of Ivan the Terrible. In 1929 it became secularized and is now a museum. Legend has it that Ivan had the architect blinded after it was completed so that it could not be replicated (and I doubt seriously if it could!). The other major tourist-attraction in Red Square was Lenin's Tomb—not nearly as colorful—but I did stand in line to get a peek at the old agitator.

After several days in Moscow we boarded the Trans-Siberian Railway for our trek across 10 time zones to Vladivostok in the Soviet Far East. This was something we were particularly looking forward to—Siberia, wow! This is a journey of over 6,000 miles and takes six to seven days if going straight through. We decided to break it up about half-way in the city of Irkutsk on beautiful Lake Baikal. Not knowing how spartan the accommodations on the train might be we reserved a private compartment (a good decision). This gave us an upper and lower bunk, a small sink and a table with two chairs under the window. It also gave us the services of who we named the "train matron." Her domain was at the end of our car next to a large samovar. We could order tea at any time of day which was always accompanied by DELICIOUS lemon cookies (I can still taste them!). Meals were something else. This was definitely not a trip for gourmands. In the late 70s, the

Soviet Union was not a tourist mecca. Their own people had food shortages. There were restaurants, but with very limited and basic fare. Art and I had been forewarned and so brought along a large jar of peanut butter which we spread liberally on the always excellent local bread. Most of the soups were also quite good, which we pretty much lived on. At the numerous station stops along the way there were usually women in babushkas on the platform offering food for sale to the passengers—often baked potatoes wrapped in newspaper (you knew you weren't on AMTRAK!)

On our fourth day we arrived in Irkutsk where we detrained for two days. Once a Cossack settlement, this city is now one of the largest in Siberia. Fortunately, it has retained much of the charm of its past—particularly its very old houses with their beautifully carved wooden shutters. The other big attraction in the area is Lake Baikal. It is the world's deepest lake (5,000 feet) and curves for nearly 400 miles through southeastern Siberia along the Mongolian border. It is frozen from December to May but since we were there in August, we were able to dip our toes in it. Yes, it was cold!

Once back on the train it was another three-plus days to Vladivostok. Throughout this entire journey, hours and hours were spent idly gazing out our window at the endless tapestry of birch trees. It was certainly not a trip for dramatic scenery. Just realizing where we were, however, gave us all the satisfaction we could wish for. Then it was in and out of Vladivostok fairly quickly. As I said earlier we had arranged to take a Japanese ship to Tokyo. It was moored at the dock when we pulled up. After boarding and being shown to our quarters (a very pleasant, if tiny, cabin) we took a look around. It didn't take long. This was a basic passenger ship. There was no swimming pool or organized entertainment and meals taken with the crew—that was the beauty of it. Sitting on deck and gazing out at the Sea of Japan as we sailed toward Tokyo for three days was wonderful. We seemed to be the only Americans aboard, and English was almost non-existent (and really quite unnecessary). All of our needs were being met, and the food was a big improvement from the Soviet Union—fresh fish being one big plus. When we arrived in Tokyo we experienced culture shock. After the "greyness" of the USSR we were met with bright lights and bustling crowds. We enjoyed this change of scene for several days before boarding our Philippine Airlines flight bound for L.A. (via Manilla). We had found this to be the least expensive way to return home. Our overnight at a hostel in Manilla provided an unexpected surprise. In the middle of the night Art's flimsy bed collapsed and he spent the rest of the night on the floor. Oh well, you get what you pay for!

CHAPTER 9

RUN GIRL RUN

MY VERY FIRST RACE TOOK PLACE WHEN I WAS 3 OR 4 ON Santa Monica Beach. It was an Easter "kiddy race." I don't remember if I won or not but I do remember being handed a big plush bunny at the finish line (which I think all the kids got). I was hooked! It wasn't until nearly 40 years later, however, in February of 1978 that I began running seriously.

Growing up in the 50s, running was not considered proper for a girl. As compensation, I remember going for long walks (sometimes up to 10 miles) through the streets of L.A. and getting a bus back home. Later, in high school, I got ready for gym class early one day and made a dash for the "boys" track. Its 440 yard oval drew me like a moth to a flame. Could I actually run all the way around without stopping? I didn't get to find out on that day since the boys' P.E. teacher yelled at me to get off the track. For a brief time after high school graduation an ex-Olympian came into my life. Stella Walsh (Stanislawa Walasiewicz) was a Polish medalist in the 1936 games in Berlin, then living in Los Angeles. A group of like-minded girls and I would meet her on the track at L.A. Valley College once a week to learn the basics of track and field. I think she realized our dilemma and offered her services for free. I became a sprinter and a "broad" jumper. I loved it! This was well before the running boom of the 70s and its introduction of distance running/jogging to the general populace. The coaching went on for several years and eventually came to an end.

Fast forward to February, 1978—the running/jogging boom had begun. The impetus was on health, not competition, thereby making it suitable for everyone (females included!). By this time I was 42. I was also a smoker—a product of my generation—but I seized the opportunity that lay ahead of me. I decided to cut down to three cigarettes a day (one after each meal). In six months, however, I was back to half-a-pack a day. Then came the day of reckoning. I would either smoke or run. Fortunately, running won out, and I ran my first marathon six months later—the Culver City Marathon (now known as the Western Hemisphere Marathon). For the next 20 years I ran approximately two marathons a year. Highlights were the first L.A Marathon in 1986, two New York City Marathons (1979 and 1986), the Paris Marathon (1984) with recovery on the island of Mykynos, the Big Sur Marathon (1988), the previously-mentioned Honolulu Marathon (1980), and the Portland Marathon (1988) which qualified me for the Boston Marathon which I ran in 1989. Boston is the only marathon where one has to qualify by bettering a time dependant on one's age-group. I made it in the 50-54 division with a 3:42. My last marathon, at age 65, was the Millennium Marathon in New Zealand in 2000. This was very special for me since the race took place in my father's birthplace, as I have previously mentioned. It was also the country where each new millennium first dawned. My friend Jan joined me on this trip. We had planned to explore some of the South Island's world-renowned hiking "tracks" after the race. Unfortunately, I had developed a "bug" on the plane coming over, and the marathon nearly did me in (although I managed to finish). Jan had to go out on her own and tell me about her "tramps" on the "tracks" while I recovered in a B & B.

About two years after I started running I became one of the founding members of the Los Angeles Frontrunners. The Frontrunners is a gay running club (now international) which had had its genesis several years earlier in San Francisco. We met in L.A.'s Griffith Park for our Saturday workouts and enjoyed delicious breakfasts afterwards. Today, there are numerous Frontrunner clubs throughout the world—a number of which I have run with, including London and Sydney. The camaraderie among the members of these clubs is fantastic. Everyone is cheered on and encouraged. Although I have lived in Eugene for the past 28 years I still maintain my membership in the L.A. club because of the friends I made almost 30 years ago, and I always try to schedule my trips to SoCal to include a Saturday morning workout in Griffith Park. I will mention one amusing anecdote. At one of these breakfasts I was seated next to a rather small man with a booming bass voice who I didn't recognize. I happened to mention, "With that voice, you should be an actor." He modestly replied, "Well, as a matter of fact, I am." Turned out it was George Takei (Mr. Sulu of Star Trek!). Red-faced, I apologized for not being a Trekkie.

Around this same time, the Gay Games came into existence founded by a gentleman by the name of Tom Waddell. They were first held in San Francisco in 1982. The Olympic folks would not sanction a "Gay Olympics," but I think Gay Games rolls off the tongue with much more panache. The games are held every four years in various parts of the world. I participated in 1986 (San Francisco), 1990 (Vancouver, B.C), 1994 (New York City), 2002 (Sydney Australia), 2006 (Chicago) and 2010 (Cologne, Germany). At the conclusion of the Cologne games I took a 4-day stroll along the Rheinsteig—a fabulous hiking trail paralleling the Rhine River which took me through villages and vineyards and past a number of fabled castles. Nights were spent at inns along the way.

I will mention one more Gay Games experience. This was in Sydney in 2002—just two years after the Olympic Games were held there. Competition took place in Olympic Park—a state-of-the-arts sports park built specifically for the Games. We would be literally running in the footsteps of the Olympians! Arriving in Sydney on Halloween, we were not met at the airport by pumpkins and witches but did see lots of welcoming signs for Gay Games participants coming into town. Since Eugene does not have a

Frontrunners club I ran with my old buddies in "Team L.A" as did my Vermonter friend Fran (since Burlington does not have a club either). We had rented a nice little apartment in King's Cross for the duration of the games. It was very convenient for exploring other parts of the city in between events and after the games. One of the best things about competing as a team is marching together into the stadium holding your team name high during opening ceremonies (just like the Olympics!). And, of course, we sported terrific uniforms.

As for the games, themselves, I was now in the 60-64 division. I entered the sprint triathlon (using a rented bike), the 200m, the 1500m, the 10K, the long jump and the 1500m swim (for a change of pace, literally). The running and jumping events went very well, and I was extremely proud to receive five gold medals. The swim not so much. In fact, I came in dead last in my division. I figured my great endurance in running would follow over into swimming—NOT! It seems that in competition swimming, technique is of the utmost importance and, unfortunately, I possessed very little, having just done lots and lots of laps in my local pool in preparation. My competitors were, no doubt, high and dry and enjoying a Toohey's poolside by the time I finished my laps! I now stick to running (competing in the 80-84 category).

Some of our "outside of the games" activities included exploring the fascinating Sydney waterfront, a cruise in gorgeous Sydney Harbor and a dip in the surf at world-famous Bondi Beach. We also hiked a bit in the nearby Blue Mountains. We had hoped to do more of this, but fire danger had closed many of the "tracks." Instead, we took a train about an hour north of Sydney to the Central Coast and spent several days beachwalking along the coast in a national park. Back in Sydney, Fran paid a visit to Ayers Rock before heading home to Vermont and I headed to Western Australia—the only part of the country I had missed during my first visit in 1969 (some 30 years earlier).

For this journey, I boarded the Indian-Pacific railway in Sydney which headed due west to Perth. This train is aptly named because it travels between the Pacific Ocean and the Indian Ocean. As it's a 3-day journey (arriving in Perth on the fourth morning), I opted for "Gold" Kangaroo service as opposed to "Red" Kangaroo service. This got me a private little cubicle and all meals. During the day I lounged comfortably in my cozy compartment and gazed out the window at the rather barren scenery. This train travels through the Nullarbor ("no trees") Plain on the longest straight stretch of track in the world. From time to time kangaroos were spotted hoping about, breaking up the monotony, as well as some beautiful eagles which could be seen as they soared near the train on occasion. After dinner a steward would come in and adjust my seat into a very comfortable bed. I have always loved sleeping on a train, especially the old steam trains where one was lulled to sleep by the clickity-click sound of the rails.

Spent three very interesting and diverse days in Perth. One of them involved a wild drive through the adjacent sand dunes in a 4-wheel drive vehicle. At one point the driver stopped and issued each of us a sand board with which we could do our own navigating—a new experience! Another day I took the ferry to Rottnest Island (12 miles west of Perth). Here I rented a bike and pedaled to a wonderful snorkeling beach. The tropical aqua blue of the water was amazing as was the pink coral below the surface. The fish were not abundant, but there were enough to make it interesting. Just before leaving the island I spotted a "quokka." This is a marsupial that lives only on Rottnest and is quite a draw for visitors. It resembles a miniature kangaroo—about a foot high and very cute! A final activity in the area was a drive through the Margaret River wine country with its several tasty stops.

My return to Sydney was by air, and once back there I had one more adventure on my calendar before returning home. This was an 18-mile, 2-day coastal walk in Royal National Park (just south of Sydney). The ocean views along this trail were gorgeous and the trail more than diverse. Sometimes I'd be clambering over rocks along the beach and sometimes walking high up on the headlands. My one night out was spent on a grassy area just above the beach. The weather was temperate, so no need for a tent. I had purchased a light weight sleeping bag to keep off the chill off threw a bit of food into my backpack—perfectly adequate for the 2-day walk. Back in Sydney, my last event of this venture was the "Moonlight Over Manhattan" concert in the Royal Botanic Gardens. What an absolute joy to sit back and listen to one after another of my favorite Broadway hits.

— CHAPTER 10 —

BACK TO THE TURNTABLE

As mentioned previously, my ties to the recording industry were cut in the late 70's. Some five years later, however, I got a call from my old boss, now at MCA Records, asking me if I would like to return to the fold. There was an opening he thought I might fill. I really had to think about it as the freedom of the "temp" lifestyle once again was suiting me quite well. Since MCA had requested my services, however, I found myself in a good bargaining position—the main point being three weeks' vacation a year. This was granted, along with a private office and a generous salary, so I accepted the offer and hopped back on the turntable. My new position was that of production manager. That meant I had to insure that all the components (master tape, album jacket materials, etc.) for each release arrived at our pressing plants in a timely manner. This was before computers and done through phone and fax. During this time I got to visit our pressing plant in Pinckneyville, Illinois and watch the whole process in motion—most interesting. I also got to run a 10K while there as one of the guys I dealt with was also an avid runner. This was in the days of LP's and cassettes, CD's not arriving on the scene until the end of my career. One of the perks of this job was that I was entitled to a copy of each release. These were the DJ "Not for Sale" copies with a hole punched in the corner of the jacket. The majority of our product I didn't much care for but I enjoyed some of the pop stuff as well as occasional reissues of old musicals from time to time. In addition, we had a pretty decent classical line. Whatever I didn't care for I took to a little "underground" shop in Hollywood and sold for anywhere from fifty cents to a dollar an album—a nice little perk!

One of the best things about this job was that I could walk to my office in Universal City. In 1968, I had bought a little Spanish-style house in North Hollywood (for $29,500), not more than a mile away, never dreaming that one day I would stroll down Lankershim Boulevard to work. My boss was a lively Estonian named Ulo. He was quite a character, and we got along splendidly. Some of our lunches were a bit "spirited," but we always seemed to get the job done. He hosted an annual Christmas party at his San Fernando Valley condo in Tarzana. One of the games we played was "pop the champagne cork into the swimming pool"- from an upstairs balcony. I have fond memories of those days, but they were not to last forever. Now it was my turn to jump off the turntable for good.

— CHAPTER 11 —

THE OREGON TRAIL

IN 1990, MCA's RECORDING DIVISION WAS TAKEN OVER BY A Japanese firm. This time I could stay on, but I didn't like how my job was going to change. I went home and thought about it and came back the next morning with my resignation. I had actually given some serious thought to moving out of L.A. with its tremendous traffic problems, just not quite this soon. I was only 55, but the more I thought about it the more excited I got about making the move.

Shortly thereafter I took a drive up to the Pacific northwest and really liked what I saw—lots of green, blue skies, and a fraction of the traffic. I checked out Seattle, Portland, and Eugene. Seattle had a gorgeous setting on Puget Sound, with the Olympic Range across the water, but it also had freeways. Portland seemed a pleasant-enough town, but Eugene seemed just right (the Goldilocks Syndrome). For me, its two major assets were the University of Oregon (and the cultural diversity it offered) and its reputation as a runners' town. By this time I was a total running junkie. I decided to rent a cheap apartment for six months and see how I liked it. December arrived while I was there. It snowed, and the temperature dropped to 5 (five!) degrees—quite a change for this Southern California girl. I loved it! I then returned to L.A., put my house on the market and hightailed it back to Eugene. Within two months I found a house on the Willamette River (which runs right through town) with a bike/running path directly outside my front door. The next chapter of my life had begun.

At age 55, I was not quite ready to retire. Since the recording industry was not exactly booming in Eugene I decided to go back to my secretarial roots. I soon discovered, however, that Oregon's economy was very different from California's. What made it wonderful for buying a house was not so great when it came to salaries. So instead of getting tied up in a permanent position at $6-8 an hour I hopped back into the temp pool where I could come and go as I chose. One of my best assignments was being sent to the Mayor and City Manager's office in Springfield (Eugene's sister city across the river). Working with then Mayor Bill Morrisette was a joy. He was a retired history teacher, avid politico, and all-around swell guy. Between my clerical duties, we had some great discussions. At that time, Springfield had an anti-gay measure on the ballot, and Bill did his best to oppose it (it lost!). Subsequent assignments took me to the area's water treatment plant, the University of Oregon's music department, and a Levi-Strauss manufacturing plant—each adding to the "google" in my brain.

— CHAPTER 12 —

THE PACIFIC CREST TRAIL

IN 1995, A HIKING FRIEND, SUSAN, CALLED AND ASKED IF I
would like to accompany her on a portion of the Pacific Crest Trail
the following year. The PCT is a 2,600 mile-long trek which tra-
verses three states (California, Oregon, and Washington) between
Mexico and Canada. It is one of three National Scenic Trails in the
U.S. A. The others being the Appalachian Trail and the Continental Divide Trail. Susan informed me that she would be turning 50
that year and was planning to backpack the Oregon portion of the
trail and would I like to join her for part of it. I had done a lot of
short-distance hiking/backpacking but nothing of this magnitude.
I thought for about ten seconds and then asked if she'd like my
company for the entire distance (some 460 miles), to which she
happily agreed. Since I would be turning 60 soon this would also
be a milestone for me. Despite some major challenges (or perhaps
because of them), I LOVED this adventure. My good friend Fran
once said that to be a successful long-distance backpacker you
have to know the difference between pain and discomfort. There
is a good deal of the latter, but so worth it. This trip inspired me to
eventually complete the entire trail.

For the next ten years I became what is known as a "section
hiker,"—completing about 250 miles a year (I soon acquired the
trail name of T.O.B., or Tough Old Broad! I did not do the trail in
geographical order, but according to the season and where I could
get support, One of the most important preparations in long-distance hiking is arranging your food supply. I could carry about a

week's worth on my back and then had to "re-supply." This meant either being met by someone at a trailhead (not easy on the more remote sections of the PCT) or mailing a food box to a post office somewhere near the route. I was fortunate to have some good friends who helped me out in the northern portions of the trail and a wonderful brother and his wife who came to my aid in some of the southerly sections. These folks often had to navigate some very marginal back roads. And they often brought me some REAL FOOD in addition to what I had put in my re-supply boxes. Day after day of ramen noodles and instant oatmeal can get very tiresome (even to a non- foodie)! Besides food concerns, weather was also a major consideration. This is probably the *prime* concern for "through-hikers"—those who hike the entire distance in one season. Starting at the California/Mexico border in late April, they have to traverse the Sierra Nevadas on their way north while they are still snow-bound. In heavy snowfall years some of these hikers leave the trail when they reach the Sierras and head up to Canada to hike south until the snow melts (these folks are called "yo-yo" hikers). As a section-hiker I could choose my seasons—such as hiking the Sierras in July or August when I could see the trail underneath my feet (my navigational skills are almost non-existent). I made a very bad logistical error one year by starting a section in the Southern California desert in mid-May. Big mistake! When the temperature reached 110-degrees I had to seek the almost non-existent shade of a joshua tree or a large boulder. I tried hiking at night, but did not feel comfortable. The night sky cast eerie shadows on the sand, and I was afraid of veering off the trail.

My two other major concerns were water sources and river crossings. As I could only hike 10-12 miles a day (about half what younger folks and the through-hikers do), I did not necessarily come across a water source each day. This meant carrying it on my back. Water is heavy! This was tough! On occasion, the only water available was that which had pooled in ruts in the trail. Strained through a bandana it served its purpose and perhaps added a little mineral content to my diet! The river crossings were another matter. Here there was too much water—usually icy-cold as it raced its way down from snow-capped mountains. At only 5'2" it didn't take much for the water to reach above my knees. This made it very difficult to move forward. Added to this, the imbalance caused by the weight of my pack made these crossings a real challenge. On a few of these sections, my friend Jan from Albuquerque joined me and was able to come to my aid at nasty crossings. At 25 years my junior, she would cross the rivers with her pack, drop it off on the other side, and then come back for mine. What a pal! Without the pack I could manage.

There were so many memorable moments on this 10-year odyssey, I will only touch on a few. One such memory involves standing atop a pass and looking out at the trail on the other side as it snaked downward. It was a beautiful, sunny afternoon, and I got to chatting with a fellow hiker. It turned out he was from Santa Barbara (the home of my brother's family) so we had a lot to chat about. In time, he began the descent while I lingered a bit longer to enjoy the vista. All of a sudden, the sky darkened with ominous clouds. This impelled me to get going. In a short time I felt rain drops, and then it began to pour. I dropped my pack to get at my rain gear (such as it was) and awkwardly put it on. Before long, the downhill path was resembling a river but was still navigable. My main concern at this point was where was I going to camp? The terrain was very unfriendly, and I was getting very wet (and cold). Thoughts of hypothermia began creeping into my mind. Then, out of the blue, I heard "Jane"! It was the guy I had talked with earlier. "Ben" truly was my savior. He had found shelter in a pile of boulders that had formed a sort-of cave. He directed me inside, told me to take off my clothes while handing me some dry stuff of his. I did as I was told and was soon curled up in my sleeping bag (in his long johns!) It took me almost an hour to get warm! At that point Ben brought me a hot dinner—what a guy! After the storm passed, and before nightfall, he took my wet clothes and draped them over some rocks to dry. They were still damp in the morning, but my body heat soon took care of that. And the hot breakfast Ben provided me with definitely helped in the warming process. I'm not sure what would have happened if he hadn't helped me. The following year I paid him a visit in Santa Barbara and we had a meal in a lovely outdoor patio with bright sunshine overhead. Another super guy I met was Evan. This was on a section I was hiking (once again) with my friend Jan and her friend Zoe—two much younger (and faster) ladies. When it became apparent that I was a good deal slower than they were, we made a plan. I would start out an hour or so ahead of them in the morning and they would catch up with me. As I was taking a break thinking I might see Jan and Zoe soon Evan walked by, slowing to say "hi," and we began to chat. He was a very fit- looking senior (probably 60ish). He lives in Ukiah, in Northern California, and regularly backpacks in the summer. As we talked we found out that we were heading for the same camp spot that day—about a mile or two up the trail—so he took off and we said we'd see each other later. Not long afterwards, my friends came by and we continued to the campsite where we found Evan. He had very good news for me. A Boy Scout troop was camped nearby, and he had talked them into carrying my pack up to one of the highest passes on the trail the next day. I had been quite concerned about this climb, and now I didn't have to worry. The Boy Scouts split my pack up so several of them earned merit badges that day for helping a "little old lady"—not to cross a street but to climb a mountain! I have since visited Evan in his home and met his very nice partner, also a hiker.

And then there was the bear scare. I was hiking a section south of Yosemite known for its ursine inhabitants. Therefore, hikers were required to pack all food and cosmetics in bear canisters (which we rented). Nobody likes them because they add about 2-1/2 pounds to our packs. Anyway, it was late afternoon and I began scouting the surrounding real estate for a place to camp. I spotted a nice-looking flat area nestled in the trees with a gurgling little river at its side—perfect! I quickly set up my tent and then sat back and reveled in the surroundings for a bit. This is one of the things I LOVE about backpacking—the very up close and personal relationship with nature. And with no one around it's sublime! Sublimity, however, soon came to a screeching halt. As I was enjoying my after-dinner coffee and writing in my journal, I suddenly sensed I was not alone any more. Peering over my left shoulder I spotted a bear not 20 feet away with its nose in my canister. I had broken a cardinal rule—never leave your bear canister open and unattended (I had planned on a little snack later before getting in my sleeping bag and so had left it open). I didn't know whether to be terrified or indignant. I still had four days to go, and my rations were being guzzled! I had heard it's a good thing to make yourself look bigger in such a situation, and at only 5'2" anything would help so I stood up, waved my arms in the air and shouted. The bear glanced at me with not much concern and after a short time, probably annoyed by my antics, ambled calmly off into the woods with some of my food dangling from its mouth. I, of course, was terribly concerned. I quickly gathered up the food that was strewn about, put it back in my canister, secured the lid, and placed it in a pile of rocks, hoping the bear would not return. I then took my sleeping bag and walked about 200 yards down the trail to spend the night. I didn't want the bear to come sniffing around my tent in the middle of the night (where I knew there must be some food odors after ten days on the trail). Shortly after hunkering down under a tree I heard the bear's return. It had found the canister and was doing its best to get it open (the way they are constructed, this is virtually impossible). This racket lasted for about 15 minutes, and then all was silent. This was worse than hearing the bear's noise because now I didn't know where it was. I was sure I wouldn't sleep a wink, but I eventually dropped off. When I awoke at first light I walked down to my campsite fully expecting the worst—tent and sleeping bag torn to shreds in the bear's food quest. But to my amazement, all was as I had left it. Except for my canister which was nowhere to be found. My thought was that the bear must have whacked it into the river in its effort to get it open. So there I was, four days to go with no food. Fortunately, this section of the Pacific Crest Trail coincides with the 225-mile-long John Muir Trail and is very well-traveled. After only a couple of hours I saw some hikers coming the other way towards me. The closer they got, the bigger they appeared. Good, I thought, the bigger they are the more food they might have to share. And so it was. They were three guys from England who just the night before had talked about having brought too much food and wanting to lighten their packs—a match made in heaven! Not only did I not have to "dine" on ramen noodles and instant oatmeal for four more days, I now had some delicious English curry dinners as well as a couple of packets of yummy Cadbury's hot chocolate mix. I was able to further supplement my larder with bits and pieces from other hikers happy to help. The long-distance hiking family is the best! The P.S. to this story is that my canister was found by some hikers about a year later washed up against the stream. They soon found out what a mistake it was to open it. The stench of its fermenting contents almost felled them! The name of the company I had rented it from was on the inside lid, and the hikers called to let them know what had happened. They, in turn, let me know the end of the story.

And now for the memory that is most seared in my mind. In 2001 Jan once again flew out from Albuquerque to join me. We started in Tuolumne Meadows (55 miles from Yosemite). The date was September 11. We decided to treat ourselves to a last real meal in the café there before heading out on the trail. While we were awaiting our bacon and eggs, an employee came into the dining room and announced the unbelievable news—the Twin Towers had been attacked. We all looked at each in stunned silence! We carried this information with us for the next two weeks, imparting the news to those we met along the trail—some had heard, some hadn't. What a message to impart to strangers!

One last thing I want to mention about the Pacific Crest Trail is the loving assistance of "trail angels". These beautiful people bring water (and sometimes other goodies) to remote sections of the trail where there are long stretches between water sources. I first came across one of these "drops" on my third day after heading north from the Mexican border. I looked ahead and thought I was seeing a mirage. Not only were there a number of water bottles on the side of the trail, but a chair to sit on and take a rest! This is truly a labor of love since accessing the trail often involves navigating "iffy" back roads. And then there were two super trail angel "rest stops." The first being "Hiker's Heaven" in Agua Dulce, California. Donna Saufley and her husband, Jeff, catered to a hiker's every need. Next to their home they offered a large grassy area on which to camp, as well as an adjacent RV with a shower and internet access. And to top it off, when you arrived you handed Donna your dirty duds (she gave you loners to put on) and later returned them all clean! The second super stop along the way was "Casa de Luna", overseen by "The Andersons," also in California. Here you got a nice space in their backyard to camp, bathroom privileges in their house, a taco salad for dinner, and pancakes the next morning before departure. And what a departure it was—the "lady of the house" stood in the front door to wave good-bye and then turned around and dropped her drawers. Hence, "Casa de Luna"!

— CHAPTER 13 —

THE CAMINO DE SANTIAGO

BY THE END OF 2010, HAVING COMPLETED THE PACIFIC CREST
Trail four years before, I began to get antsy for another long-distance
trek. I had heard bits and pieces about the Camino de Santiago in
(primarily) Spain and began doing some research. I learned that the
most popular route started in St-Jean-Pied-de-Port in France and
headed some 500 miles almost directly west to the city of Santiago
in Spain. Santiago is a pilgrimage city for Catholics as the bones of St.
James (Santiago) are purported to be buried there. Catholic or not,
folks who undertake this trek are called "peregrinos" (pilgrims), and
I decided I wanted to be one of them. The trip had to be postponed
until 2012, however, as I unfortunately fractured a hip in the spring
of 2011 when jumping off a bus onto a very wet street in Eugene.
Fortunately, my recovery went well, and the trip was rescheduled to
the fall of 2012. In the meantime I endeavored to find a similarly-in-
clined old-lady adventurer to join me. At 75, I had few takers (let's
say none), so I consulted the Pacific Crest Trail website and placed
an ad—"Looking for older woman to join me in walking the Camino
de Santiago." The one response I got stated, "I am not a woman and
do not want to hike the Camino, BUT...Turned out it was from a
Frenchman who lived near the Pyrenees in France—not far from the
start of the Camino. He was an avid hiker who was very familiar with
the Pacific Crest trail and often checked out their website. Lucky me!
"Philippe" offered me the hospitality of his home before and after the
walk as well as a lift to the trailhead. So, on September 8, 2012 I got
off the train in Pau, at the foot of the Pyrennes, where my benefactor

was waiting for me. A 15-minute drive took us to his lovely home. His wife, Anne-Marie was not home. She not only works as a physician full-time at the local hospital, but is a "Doctor without Borders" in her "spare" time. She was off on a mission of mercy when I arrived, but I was very happy to meet her the following year when I returned. Philippe had just retired as a professor of American Studies at the local university, so his English was "*tres bien.*" This was good because my French was "*tres mal.*" After two wonderful days in Pau he drove me to the start of the Camino in St-Jean. Here I got my "pilgrim's passport" which allowed me to stay in the *albergues* (hostels) along the route at a very modest rate (about $8.00 a night). The passports were duly stamped at each *albergue* to verify completion at the end of the trail in Santiago. Here, one received an impressive-looking certificate of completion (which hangs in my living room).

On the auspicious day of September 11 the journey began which would end up 40 days later at the cathedral in Santiago. My pack was light—containing only a change of clothes, some toiletries, a small towel, a couple of books and some snacks to munch on along the way. No tent necessary since I would be sleeping indoors. Only a light-weight sleeping bag was needed to put atop the bunks in the *albergues*. One item which I didn't bring along, however, was earplugs (big mistake!) Some of the *albergues* held up to 50 pilgrims, so there was definitely more than a *little* night music! Smaller facilities might only have 6 to a room, but all it takes is one snorer! Oh well, that's part of the camaraderie of the pilgrimage. Food was available in the various towns and villages we passed through, at either restaurants or grocery stores. I tended to live mainly on beef jerky, bread, cheese, yogurt and fruit. In the evening I often joined other pilgrims for dinner at a local restaurant. Many had "Pilgrim Specials" at a reduced price—yea! Water was always available at the local fountains (no purification necessary) in the villages or elsewhere in bigger burgs. And, of course the day was never complete without a couple of *café con leches* and a couple of *vino tintos*. Wine was the cheapest beverage available—about 50 cents a glass!

I began this adventure with only the desire of completing another long-distance walk, but I got so much more out of it. I wasn't just a hiker out on my own. I was a pilgrim among other pilgrims with the same commitment—to walk to Santiago (Catholic or not!). Our shared desire was palpable. We could be identified by a shell we wore around our neck or attached to our backpack. Mine is now hanging on a wall in my den. This was the symbol of St. James (Santiago) and was also pictured on the directional signs along the way. Although I didn't usually start out the day walking with anyone, I would team up with folks from time to time, and we'd share experiences as we walked. Or perhaps I would join someone who was taking a break and start up a conversation. There were people from all over the world. Fortunately, the majority of them spoke at least a little English. One woman who definitely spoke English was a nun from England. We slept side by side in one of the more primitive *albergues*. The structure appeared to be a barn. Inside, there was a platform for pilgrims to place their sleeping bags. One just took the next spot when they arrived. I was fortunate to get a spot next to Sister Elizabeth and learn a bit about her life. She was a cloistered nun living in a "silent" convent, but on this journey she was allowed to speak (it would have been really difficult for her otherwise!). I learned she had always had a love of travel and that the convent had given her permission to make the pilgrimage to Santiago. This is a huge accomplishment in the Catholic Church, and I'm sure she brought great honor to her convent for completing it. You would never have known she was a nun from her appearance except for the long skirt she wore along with her sturdy hiking boots (no wimple!) We had an excellent conversation while at the *albergue*, but the next morning went our separate ways. I ran into her again several days later, however. As I was I walking through a town I heard a knock on the window of a restaurant and there was Sister Elizabeth beckoning me to come in. So I joined her for a meal and more good conversation. One of the joys of the

Camino is meeting people, parting ways, and then running into them again further down the road. It's like meeting an old friend, with delighted hugs and often a *vino tinto* if there is a bar nearby.

The trail, itself, is not particularly difficult. The hardest day is the first—heading over the mountains into Spain. Then it is pretty much rolling with only a few significant ups and downs. With no switchbacks, however, the downhills were quite wearing on my less-than-youthful knees. The majority of the Camino is in rural areas, but it does go through a few cities—Pamplona, being one, where I met up with some more familiar faces. We shared a meal together in a large plaza where Hemingway once strolled. Navigating through cities was a bit tricky. You weren't sure where to look for the trail signs. They could be on a curb, a tree, or a store window. I got momentarily lost leaving Pamplona , but just asked a local *"Donde esta el Camino? ,"* and was soon set right. Everyone along the route knows where the path is.

When I was about half-way through, I realized that I would not be able to finish in the amount of time I had allotted in order to make my flight back to the States—those darn downhills! I, therefore, decided to cut out a 100-mile section called the *meseta* (a flat, dry area I wasn't particularly looking forward to) and return the following year to complete it. This was easy to do since there was bus and train service nearby the route connecting towns and villages. Jumping ahead put me in the town of Leon. From here I would have a little over 200 miles to Santiago—about 20 days. Highlights of this section included a challenging (but well worth it) climb to the highpoint of the trip—the very quaint hamlet of O Cebreiro (4,000 feet) with its stunning views (in good weather). The weather seemed to cooperate as I passed through this Celtic region, and the vistas were truly breathtaking. A lasting memory was leaving the *albergue* on a very misty morning and looking out at the low-lying clouds hanging on either side of the trail. I felt as if I could almost reach out and touch them—quite magical!

Another highlight of this section was meeting Denise—a 52-year-old from Nebraska who had just finished a 3-year stint in the Peace Corps. Naturally, we immediately hit it off and walked together for the next several days. On the gustatory side of things, she introduced me to a new taste treat when we went to a *pulpería* whose specialty is octopus! It was served on a wooden platter sliced and breaded—very well-seasoned with paprika and garlic. Toothpicks were used to skewer the morsels. This delicacy was accompanied by a large basket of bread and a bottle of wine—yum!

The night before reaching Santiago was filled with anticipation (and not much sleep). What a feeling to walk into town and come face to face with the fabled cathedral—a truly amazing sight shining in the morning light. As soon as I entered I got in a long line waiting to climb a stairway leading up to a statue of Santiago in the front of the cathedral. If you have completed the pilgrimage it is customary to hug the statue and give thanks for having done so. James (Iago) was a bit rotund for me to get my arms around, but I gave it my best shot while giving him my sincere thanks. Next was a pilgrims' mass. This mass takes place every day at noon, and since it was a Sunday the place was packed! The highlight of the mass was the swinging of an immense censer—definitely not what you would find in your neighborhood church! It hung from ropes in the ceiling and was swung from one side of the cathedral to the other by a number of priests. I then walked to the nearby *peregrino* office to claim my certificate of completion—a very impressive document written in Latin (with even my name translated into Latin). And who should I run into, but Denise! She had already booked a room at a place she liked, so I followed her back and booked one for myself. That evening we had a fabulous dinner with other *peregrinos* we had met along the way. What did I say about old home week? Although reaching Santiago is considered the official end of the journey, a little icing on the cake is to go on to Finisterre—a small port town on the Atlantic some 75 miles west of Santiago and dip your toes in the Atlantic. The ancients thought this was the end of the earth (hence its name). You actually get a special certificate if you do this extra bit on foot but I didn't feel I needed it (400 miles was quite enough!). So I took a very pleasant bus ride to this picturesque little spot. Found a very nice room overlooking the town's red tile roofs and the sea beyond where I enjoyed my *tinto* while watching the sun set over the water. Then, the next morning I took off on foot again for the 2-day walk up the coast to Muxia. This is the place where the Virgin Mary was said to have arrived in a stone boat—common transport of the day—to hear Iago preach (and perhaps help him with his Christianising with which he was having a bit of trouble). There is a sanctuary there called *Nuestra Senora de la Barca (Our Lady of the Boat)* which I wanted to see. The route was not all that well marked, and I had some difficulty staying on course. I finally resorted to a hitch which took me right into town. My driver recommended the Bela Muxia *albergue*, and it was, indeed "bela"—very modern and with a cat in its logo (which greatly pleased me). They sold merchandise with this logo so of course I had to buy a mug which brings back wonderful memories every time I use it. The following day I started out from town to walk to Muxia's farthest point of rocky headland where the sanctuary is located. And who should I run into but Sister Elizabeth who was headed the same way. What an amazing coincidence! Who better to share the experience with but a Catholic nun. When we reached the sanctuary, we simply stood silently side by and allowed ourselves to be immersed in our own special thoughts. I can't imagine a better way to end this venture. After leaving Muxia I made my way back to Philippe's home in Pau via bus and train. What great memories I had to keep me company. Then it was the train to Paris and flight back to the States.

I returned the following year in May to do the "*meseta*"—the 100-mile section between Burgos and Leon which I had skipped the year before. This time I was accompanied by my long-time running buddy Frank who is also an avid hiker, in addition to being my CPA! As an aside: Frank's wife, Beverly, is my treasured cat-sitter without whom I could not go on my adventures! We flew to Madrid since we were picking up the trail about half-way across Spain. After overnighting in the city we would then have about a 2-hour bus ride to our starting point in Burgos. Madrid is a wonderful town—lots of old-world charm as well as a very up-beat atmosphere. We arrived in the morning quite sleep-deprived and made our way from the airport to the Puerto del Sol metro stop—a neighborhood suggested by Rick Steves as being charming and economical. We found it to be both and soon located a swell room with private bath for about US $60.00 After stashing our stuff we then decided to stay up rather than crash. We explored our neighborhood winding up at an outdoor "*tapas bazaar*" in the late afternoon. These yummy treats were set up on table after table under a huge tented area. You simply pick up a plate and stroll from one table to another sampling whatever strikes your fancy while sipping a glass of vino if desired. We returned to the hotel about 9 p.m. and THEN crashed!

The following morning we made our way to Burgos and set foot on the Camino. What a joy I felt to be back on this fabled path, and Frank, too, seemed to feel the excitement. We had gotten our pilgrim's passports ahead of time so were more than ready to head out. Since we had about 100 miles to go, we planned on walking 10 miles a day for 10 days which actually worked out just fine. Frank was younger and faster than I was so he would usually walk ahead, particularly in the latter part of the day, so as to secure beds for us in the next *albergue* (occasionally they would fill up). One of my fondest memories is entering the next town or village and seeing Frank walking towards me with a *cerveza* (very refreshing after a long walk!). Although the *meseta* was mostly flat and straight, it still offered the lure of progress as we looked ahead in the distance and found landmarks to head for. Again, the highlight of the trail was the meeting and re-connecting of pilgrims at various points along the way. People soon got to know the duo of Frank and Jane.

At the end of our odyssey, we made our way back by train to visit Philippe in Pau. I wanted Frank to meet this wonderful guy I had met the previous year. And, once again, he was waiting on the platform to greet us. Spent two days relaxing in his lovely home and, this time, his Doctor Without Borders wife Anne-Marie was there as well. What a delight to meet her. Not only is she (I assume) a good doctor, but she is also a good cook! I particularly remember a delicious salmon and rice casserole topped off by an absolutely yummy strawberry cheesecake. After two very pleasant days, Philippe drove us to the airport in Lourdes to catch a plane to Barcelona. Neither Frank nor I had been to that city, so being that it was only 45 minutes away (by air), we decided to have a look—a good decision. Upon landing we took a taxi straight to our hotel—not being familiar with the local public transportation. After checking in we went out to have a look around. Our hotel was right in the center of things, and since it was now around 5:00, our tummies suggested we look around for a place to eat—certainly not a dinner house as Spaniards don't even *think* about dinner until after 9:00. *Tapas*, though, are something else and available much earlier. We found a place called *Tapa Tapas* adjacent to the bull ring. It looked quite inviting and was very crowded (a good sign). We ordered our *tapas* and a beer—a bit on the expensive side but well worth it for the atmosphere. In fact, we were enjoying ourselves so much that we had a second round of both *tapas* and beer. There was supposed to be a "Dancing Egg" celebration in front of the bull ring but it never happened. Around 8:00 we took the subway (the Diagonal Line) back to our hotel.

The next couple of days in Barcelona were filled with wonderful explorations. We got on to the subway system easily, maybe too easily. Frank and I bought a transit card and shared it. He would go through the turnstyle and then hand the card back for me to use. At one station, just as we got through the turnstyle we saw the train pulling in, so we ran to get on and were immediately enveloped by bodies. Later that day Frank reached for his wallet and found it was not there. We figured the thief had seen Frank put the transit card back in his wallet after I handed it to him, watched where he put it, and then followed him onto the train and made the heist (totally unnoticed in the crowded conditions). We were much more discreet in our card-sharing thereafter. Later, we were told that this station was one of the most pick-pocketed stations in Barcelona—oh, well, *asi es la vida*!

A visit to Barcelona is certainly not complete without becoming aware of Antoni Gaudi's pervasive architectural presence in the city. Gaudi is renowned for what is called Catalan Modernism—his curvy facades probably being the most prominent feature of his work. Our round of activities included a visit to his most celebrated structure—*La Sacrada Familia* (a tribute to the Holy Family)—begun in 1882 and not expected to be completed until 2026! We did not go inside as the line was prohibitive, but the exterior alone filled us with amazement. It was interesting to note that some Islamic influences can also be found in Gaudi's work. After several great days in Barcelona, we hopped on the train for the 2-3/4 hour ride north to Madrid—our departure point for the U.S. We had arranged to stay at the same nice little pension we had stayed upon arrival in the country some two weeks earlier. We even got our same comfortable room. As our flight left the next morning, we had one last meal in that lovely city, and would you believe we ran into two "pilgrims" at an all-you-can eat-buffet near our hotel. How lovely to have our "last supper" together. Talk about serendipity!

— CHAPTER 14 —

WALKING HOLIDAYS IN THE U.K.

Western Way and Burren Way—Ireland

THE SUMMER OF 2007 FOUND ME AND MY ERSTWHILE WALK-
ing buddy, Fran, on the west coast of Ireland. We had signed up with
a U.K. outfit to have a look at this part of the world. The Western
Way is part of a major walking route that will one day go round
the entire country. This was a group trip where we walked with
other hikers approximately 60 miles in 6 days (with one rest day),
stopping at pre-booked inns each night. This is a most civilized way
to go for a long walk without those pesky backpacks!

Our trek began in Galway, the second largest county in Ireland,
the western part of which is largely undeveloped and where much
of the population converses in Celtic. Fortunately, our guides spoke
perfect English, albeit with a bit of a brogue. Our journey began at the
foot of Croagh Patrick, which is considered Ireland's holy mountain.
It was originally a Druid place of worship, but when Patrick arrived
he replaced the pagan ritual with a Christian one (for better or for
worse). We climbed this special mountain with ever-broadening
views of Clew Bay and its hundreds of islands to the west nestled in
the beautiful blue waters. After visiting the chapel at the summit, we
rested a bit and then made our way back down.

Consequent days took us through forests—often with boggy
sections—quiet country roads, and along Ireland's only fiord on
the shores of Kilary Harbour. The contrast of mountain and coastal

walking was especially enjoyable. For the most part it was easy with only a few somewhat challenging bits. Our last day's walk put us on the Burren Way, known for its rugged coastline, dramatic cliffs and magnificent wild flower-decorated limestone terraces. We first followed the coastline and later walked around the remains of deserted villages, winding up the day at the Ballvnalacken tower house—magnificently sited at edge of a cliff. This is where we spent the last night of our wonderful walk, bidding adieu to our fellow wanderers the following morning.

Fran and I extended this trip a bit by renting a car and heading out on our own for a week or so. I was a bit concerned about driving on the "wrong side" of the road, but most of the roads in Ireland are so narrow (except for the motorways) you can't really go fast enough to get into trouble. We began our trip by heading to the Dingle Peninsula which juts 30 miles out into the Atlantic. Its coastline consists of steep sea-cliffs broken by sandy beaches and has some of the best surfing in Ireland. We, however, stuck to the road. Starting at Dingle town, our entry into the peninsula took us over Conor Pass, the country's highest mountain pass. From there, it was just one dramatic scene after another—from ancient ruins to drop-dead views. At one point we came across what are now known as the "beehive huts." These structures were erected in the early Christian period taking the form of a circle of successive strata of stone, each strata lying a little closer to the center than the one beneath until only a small aperture was left at the top which could be closed with a single small flagstone, or "capstone." At another point we passed the place where some of the filming of Ryan's Daughter took place. What a wonderfully-interesting and diverse day this was! Over-population will (presumably) never be a problem here. Only tiny villages lie west of Dingle town. The sheep population, however, tops 500,000—ewes rock!

Just south of the Dingle Peninsula lies the Ring of Kerry, our next destination. This is an 111-mile circular route that has attracted visitors for hundreds of years—so why not us? Here we were treated to more gorgeous views and some of Europe's finest beaches (no swimming, but we enjoyed our lunch on one of them as we passed through). Other highlights on this drive included stopping by some Iron Age forts and later taking in a landscape carved out of rock by the last Ice Age some 10,000 years ago—pretty impressive!

Our next to last destination before we returned the car was a visit to Blarney Castle to plant a smooch on its famous stone. The locals have a very good thing going This privilege costs U.S tourists some US$20 (in 2007), but it was definitely worth it for the bragging rights. This "privilege" involves a considerable climb—127 steps to the top of the castle tower. Once there, you lean over rather awkwardly to deliver the kiss. Legend has it that this act is supposed to endow the kisser with the gift of gab. My recollection is that Fran passed on this. Perhaps she felt chatty enough!

My very last Irish experience was definitely unique—a seaweed bath (which Fran also declined). Being a confirmed "bath person" I had to try this. The bathhouse was a simple building right on the beach. One is provided with a small towel and ushered into one of the bathrooms where hot sea water pours onto a pile of black seaweed in the tub. Once I got in and the tub filled, the seaweed floated around me, releasing a thin glutinous jelly turning the water into a hot silky gel. This was a rather strange (but quite pleasant), sensation. When I got out, I never felt so smooth. Take note all you commercial skin care manufacturers!

On leaving the UK, Fran and I went our separate ways (she home to Vermont, me to Oregon). I made a pit stop in New York, catching two Broadway plays—"The Year of Magical Thinking" with Vanessa Redgrave (a classic) and "The 25th Annual Putnam County Spelling Bee" (delightfully entertaining).

Pembrokeshire Coast Path—Wales

———

TEN YEARS LATER, IN SEPTEMBER OF 2017, FRAN AND I ONCE again teamed up for a long distance walk—this time in Wales. The

Pembrokeshire Coast Path meanders 180 miles along the west coast of Wales, lying almost entirely within the Pembrokeshire Coast National Park We opted for a 7-day stretch with a goal of walking approximately 10 miles a day. Much of the path keeps to the cliff-tops affording stunning views of the Irish Sea. But along with these splendid views come fierce winds. There is nothing to block their force as they sweep in, unimpeded, across the sea from Ireland. I often had to stop, bend down, and stand my ground against the strong gusts. When not cliff-walking, we dropped sharply down from time to time to beautiful sandy beaches, picturesque harbors and little fishing villages.

We arranged this independent walk through a UK company. You simply tell them how many days you want to walk and how many miles a day you want to go. They then make lodging reservations as close to your preferred schedule as possible (in our case it worked out almost perfectly). All you have to carry is a day pack. Your luggage is transported each day to the next accommodation. This is a wonderful system. When you arrive at your destination, you are shown immediately to your room where you can relax and clean up a bit. Then off to the local pub for food and drink. Our program included breakfast, but not dinner. This was fine with us as it gave us the opportunity to mingle with the locals.

Traveling from opposite sides of the U.S., Fran and I met up in the tiny town of Sandy Haven in Wales the night before the start of the walk. Registration at this establishment was very casual. I arrived first and walked in the front door to find a note on a counter directing us to our room (no human). Shortly thereafter Fran arrived, and we strolled around the pleasant grounds which had a lovely, if somewhat distant, view of the sea. Dinner that night was "mint lamb-burgers" and a delicious side salad at a very friendly (and helpful) local pub. We had purchased a cell phone on arrival and weren't quite sure how to operate it. An accommodating young man soon set us straight.

The following morning the proprietor showed up and fixed us a very good breakfast (from which I managed to stash a yogurt and piece of fruit into my backpack for lunch). By this time several other walkers had appeared in the dining room, and we chatted amiably while enjoying our meal. The day started off with a detour due to high tides in the vicinity, and this added an extra few miles to our day's journey. Never mind—the scenery was all gorgeous—and it felt great to be on our way. We soon got our first taste of the cliff-top winds and hunkered down accordingly. This day, like those to follow, was a mix of cliff-walking (with fantastic sea views), per-ambulating across grassy fields (often populated with sheep), and a sharp descent or two to sea level (and back up again!).

Half-way through our walk, we took a rest day in St. David's. St. David's, known as the religious capital of Wales, is the country's smallest city. It has, however, one of its most prominent cathedrals—the interior of which is magnificently decorated. As we were taking in this magnificence, we were suddenly treated to even more mag-nificence—the amazing sounds of a pipe organ filling the edifice. This instrument was installed to commemorate the millennium. I must say this was one of my most memorable "clerical" experiences. On the walk back to our lodgings we stopped at the office of "Voy-ages of Discovery" and booked a trip around Ramsey Island (just offshore from St. David's) for the following day. This is a favorite spot for grey seal "pupping" and we had arrived at the perfect time to get a look at these newly-born little guys (and gals). Although our timing was good, the weather here is always "iffy." The boats do not go out if it's too rough, but conditions just barely made the cut this day and we were good to go. There were 12 of us aboard a rubber raft which was equipped with a *very* powerful engine, and we took off like a bat out of hell—eliciting shrieks from many of the unsuspecting passengers (including *moi*). Heading towards Ramsey Island at great speed we slowed down to a snail's pace once we got close to shore and then circled the island in an effort to spot the newborns. They were difficult to see because they were so very small and blended in so well with their environment, but it was fun heading in and out of the island's coves trying to spot them. We did, however, see lots of parents who looked terribly appealing as they swam close by with their heads just above the surface.

At this point in our journey Fran and I realized we would have to have a bit of "help" making our daily mileage (the wind and severe ups and downs were taking their toll). So we decided to avail ourselves of the "Puffin Express"—a local bus service almost paralleling our path. This "hitch" allowed is to shave 2-3 miles off our daily walk, and since the drivers knew where all the trailheads were, transitioning to the path was no problem. This was definitely the right move since our literature mentioned that the last half of the walk was more challenging than the first.

Indeed, as we continued north, we soon found ourselves navigating a number of especially steep downhills (I had to slide down on my butt a couple of times). After which, of course, followed very steep uphills. Back on the cliff-tops, however, where the walking was much easier, we met a number of locals out on the path taking their dogs for "walkies," some of whom seemed quite impressed with Fran's and my endeavor. Their dogs, however, not so much! It was lovely to see so many locals utilizing this national path (which is adjacent to many of the villages).

Our next to last day involved taking a wrong turn at one point, but we soon realized the error of our ways and got back on track. Not before enjoying lunch in a shaded forest glen along a lovely little creek, however, Our endpoint for the day was Newport, a town that experiences great tidal fluctuations. As we approached, we looked out upon a great expanse of sand fronting the town. A number of people and dogs were out walking and running about, and a lot of boats were resting on their bottoms awaiting the next tide. I have never seen anything quite like this. After a little confusion locating our lodgings for the night—the Golden Lion pub—we settled in and soon went downstairs for our last dinner in Wales (we would part ways the next day before dinner). For once we were not penurious with our pounds. I had a delicious Thai chicken curry dish and Fran feasted on succulent lamb chops. A very tasty way to end our trek.

The next morning we both boarded a train—I was headed to London and Fran to the airport in Manchester where she would fly home to Vermont. I had one more adventure in store—two days in London (one of my favorite cities). Arriving at Paddington Station I bought an Oyster card for my transportation needs (tube and buses) and quickly found a hotel nearby—60 pounds (US$85). This is an area I knew from past experience had some reasonable lodging. The area looked somewhat familiar even after several decades. London doesn't change much! Once settled in my room, I uncorked a bottle of wine and began to plan my itinerary—what a grand feeling to be back in Londontown once again!

The following morning I descended three floors to the basement breakfast room where the complimentary "full English breakfast" was served. This includes 2 eggs, a hefty portion of bacon (which is more like ham), stewed tomatoes, potatoes and a dab of black pudding (don't ask!). And, of course, toast in the ubiquitous toast rack which insures that your toast cools down as you eat. It's the English way! On tap for that morning was a "London Walk." These tours, which I discovered when I was here 50 years ago, are still going on. You meet at different tube stops where a local guide acquaints you with the neighborhood in a 2-hour or so walk. These folks have an intimate knowledge of their area and seem to take great joy in sharing it with visitors. And the price is right—2 pounds for seniors. The walks are theme-based, i.e. Royal London , Hidden London, Haunted London, etc. A very popular one is Jack the Ripper's London. I opted for the somewhat less sensational "Walk through Soho," although this did take us briefly through the red light district and a peek at its offerings it also gave us a great overview of the arty neighborhood. On the cultural side, houses where Mozart and Karl Marx once lived were pointed out. That afternoon I spent at the cinema enjoying the newly-released "Victoria and Abdul" with Judy Dench (one of my very favorite actresses). Watching this

English-inspired movie in London gave me quite a thrill. A lovely walk through Hyde Park at twilight ended my London Experience.

The next morning (after another full English breakfast) I boarded the Heathrow Express from Paddington to catch my flight home. This would be a new experience for me—flying business class. When I learned there was a direct flight from London to Portland I splurged (and I mean *splurged*) on this ticket. I decided I would much rather nap and eat my way back home than be crunched in coach. I loved the directional signs at the airport that read "Upper Class!" When I got to the departure lounge it was amazing. There were cushy chairs and sofas tastefully arranged plus a bountiful buffet with just about anything you might want to eat. Oh, why did I eat that full breakie at the hotel! I hadn't known what I was in for. I did manage a couple Bloody Marys before take-off, however, which put me in a pleasant mood. Once on board I found that my seat opened up fully and I could stretch out when the time came. There was no one next to me—just an area to put stuff and my table. Meals and drinks arrived at intervals. I could get used to this! After landing in Portland I hopped a shuttle bus to Eugene—home sweet home.

— CHAPTER 15 —

SOUTH AMERICA

Argentina, Chile and Patagonia

IN THE 1980'S, WHILE STILL LIVING IN L.A., I JOINED A SMALL
adventure group on a journey to Argentina and Patagonia. We
planned city sightseeing in Buenos Aires followed by some exploration and hiking in Patagonia. I can truly say that Buenos Aires
is the "Paris of South America" having sampled the original one.
It is a beautiful city, fortunately for our group, the exchange rate
at this time was very favorable to Americans. Rooms were around
$15.00 and steak dinners around $1.50. The only thing I didn't care
for was the late dining preferred by the locals. Anything before 9
p.m. would be considered an "Early Bird Special." After visiting the
Casa Rosada (presidential palace) and other city highlights, we flew
south to Ushuaia at the tip of the continent. This town overlooks
the Beagle Channel—a strait in the Tierra del Fuego archipelago
through which Darwin navigated his ship, the *Beagle,* during his
1831 voyage of exploration. It was quite a thrill to stand on this spot
looking south towards the next big land mass—Antarctica! While
in of Patagonia (comprised of southern Argentina and Chile), we
did a little hiking in the southern Andes and then hopped on a
bus for a look at the Torres del Paine in Chile. Here, we were awed
by the soaring mountains with mile-high granite towers (*torres*).
And the electric-blue of the glaciers was awesome as was the sound
when they calved into the water below. Leaving the "official" group
after two weeks, I extended the trip on my own by flying up to
Iguasu Falls on the border of Argentina and Brazil for a look at this

world-renowned natural wonder. The taxi driver said I could find a very nice "American" room for about $10. If that were the case I knew I could find a perfectly "good" one for less. Indeed, I found a swell little place for $4.00. The "shower" was a pipe sticking out of the bathroom wall where one had to squat to wash up, but that was O.K.—the water was hot! The bougainvilleas outside my window were gorgeous and made up for any minor inconveniences. The falls were almost indescribable. They are nearly twice as high as Niagara and three times as wide. When Eleanor Roosevelt paid a visit here she is reported to have said, "Poor Niagara."

The Amazon and Machu Pacchu

A SECOND TRIP TO SOUTH AMERICA TOOK PLACE IN THE early 90's after I had moved to Eugene. I noted an ad in the local paper advertising a trip to the Amazon and Machu Picchu with a University of Oregon professor acting as one of the guides. How could I resist? We flew to Lima, and then took a short hop to Iquitos. This city on the banks of the upper Amazon is the gateway to river exploration on the west side of the country. We arrived in town after dark and then boarded an open-air bus which took us to a "jungle lodge" on the bank of the river for the night—what a blend of sights and scents as we made our way through town to the riverbank. Passsing houses, we got a good look at the locals preparing dinner by the light of lanterns and got occasional whiffs of their cuisines! The next morning we boarded the boat—our home for the next week. It was definitely not a luxury craft, more akin to "The African Queen"—just my cup of tea! Since I was a single, I got the space at the very front of the vessel. It was a tiny triangle with just enough room for my bunk. But it also had a door I could open and listen to the sounds of the jungle at night or gaze out of during the day at the incredibly lush, verdant scenery. Food was definitely fresh. The cook kept a pen of chickens on deck which were dispatched as needed, and fish was caught daily. Not to mention the delicious tropical fruits. As I said, the boat was our hotel. We took excursions on smaller crafts as we explored some of the tributaries—sometimes passing lily pads measuring 20 feet or more across! Now and then we would set foot in a village where I traded several of my running T-shirts for a few unique hand-crafted items. I love to think about the locals running around in "New York City Marathon" garb, or whatever. After the Amazon, we flew to Cuzco for the next phase of our adventure—Machu Picchu. When we arrived in the city we were whisked to our hotel, given a cup of coca tea and sent to our rooms to rest. These procedures were meant to help us acclimatize to Cuzco's 11,000 ft. elevation. Fortunately, I don't seem to have a problem with altitude. Cuzco is a wonderful old city. It was once the capital of the Inca empire. Evidence of this civilization is still visible today—primarily in the walls which one comes across in various parts of town. These walls are composed of giant granite blocks carved to fit together without mortar. It's interesting to think of how many earthquakes they may have withstood. After two days exploring this historic city, we hopped on a train for Machu Picchu. We first headed uphill noting the marginal housing on either side of the tracks. The higher up one lives, the more primitive the housing. This is because it becomes a longer and longer walk to town for necessities. Eventually we reached a plateau and began heading downhill (Machu Picchu is actually 3,000 feet lower than Cuzco). Before long we arrived at a RR station on the banks of the Urumbaba River where we disembarked. Some people overnight in this town and take a day-trip to Machu Picchu the next morning. Our group, however, was fortunate to be overnighting in Machu Picchu, itself, so as to experience dawn in this legendary spot. The 57-mile-long train-ride up to the ruins takes about 3-1/2 hours and is quite a marvel of engineering. Stepping off onto the sacred grounds and looking around at scenes I'd only seen on film was breathtaking. We were taken to our hotel for a brief rest and then were off on foot to explore our unique surroundings. One of the main attractions is a calendar built around 1450 which is aligned with the sun's position during the winter solstice—my birthday! In the late 16th century, Spanish clergy considered such artifacts to have pagan implications and destroyed those they came across. Fortunately, this one escaped their notice and was found intact in 1911 when the area was re-discovered. The following morning was truly indescribable. To stand outside in the silence of the pre-dawn and watch this historic sanctuary gradually take form is something I shall never forget.

Venezuela I

A THIRD TRIP TO THIS CONTINENT TOOK PLACE IN THE SPRING of 2004. In 2003, at a long-distance hikers' conference near Portland, I got to talking with a fellow hiker/adventurer who was currently working at the American Embassy in Caracas. I happened to mention that I had never been to Venezuela. Long story short—the next year she and her husband met me at the Caracas airport for a visit. The airport is situated on the coast about 20 miles from town. The route to the city took us through a barrio. The residents here have electricity (very primitive wiring strung on ramshackle poles) but no running water. On the other hand, Bill and Carol's apartment was luxurious. It was situated on a hillside overlooking the city below. All I can say is that the U.S. government certainly doesn't seem to stint on State Department employees' housing. I had my own very attractive room and bath. While Carol tended to business at the embassy, her husband, Bill, who was retired, stayed home and turned out lightweight backpacking gear—a sewing machine was positioned at one end of the dining room table.

At this time there was considerable unrest with the Chavez regime in Caracas. Therefore, it was felt that it would probably be best if I were to do the majority of my sightseeing outside of the city. That way I would avoid possible road closures due to protests.

No actual violence was predicted, but they didn't want me to waste my time waiting out a protest. Their travel agent arranged a 10-day excursion with a private guide and car (for use when we weren't walking or trying to stay put on the back of a mule—OMG!).

Our first destination was Merida, at the base of the Andes, which is known for its Spanish colonial architecture and the prestigious *Universidad de los Andes*. We had a lovely tour of this city and then headed our vehicle uphill (and I mean *uphill*!) to *Los Nevados* (literally meaning snow-covered)—a small settlement in the Andes. The extremely rutted and curvy road was the worst I had ever been on except for the road to Lesotho—a high-altitude town in Southern Africa. It took about four rocking and rolling hours to get there. Everywhere you go in *Los Nevados* is either up or down. There is almost no level ground. After being shown to my room, which was "adequate," I hung out (literally) on a front porch hammock and soaked in the fabulous views. When I attempted to take a shower later, however, the situation was definitely not "adequate." There were two shower rooms each consisting of a small cubicle with a shower head sticking out of one corner leaving only a very small area with a chair in the opposite corner to place one's towel and clean clothes. After stripping down I turned the faucet and nothing happened. I then partially redressed, gathered up all my stuff and went next door to the other cubicle. This time when I turned the handle water came out but it was cold (we had been told there would be hot water). Quickly covering my nakedness again, I left the room and sought help. I found a guy who came in and turned a handle well above the shower head, out of my reach. Ah ha—hot water! But not for long. In the middle of washing my hair it turned cold again. Oh well, I do not travel looking for great bathrooms, but for new experiences—and this was one of them! The mule ride was another. This half-day excursion took us down a steep trail to a river below. The lush vegetation was gorgeous. The physical challenge of staying on top of a mule going steeply downhill was something else! I had to lean back in the saddle to keep my balance and not topple over the mule's head. Coming back up was just as bad. I had to lean forward—all the while holding on to my saddle horn in a death grip—to keep from falling backwards. I am definitely not an experienced muleteer! The scenery, however, as previously stated, was lovely!

After two days in *Los Nevados* we headed back down the God-awful road to Merida and then on to *Los Llanos* (the plains). A different car and driver awaited me for this segment. The weather at this much lower elevation was a great deal warmer—in fact, hot! Unfortunately, the car did not have air-conditioning. I was praying that my next lodgings would have a proper bathroom with functioning hot and cold water. I needn't have worried. The *Posada Dona Barbara* ranch was strictly first class. Within minutes of our arrival I was lounging on my king-sized bed in an air-conditioned room sipping a refreshing glass of sangria (compliments of the house). Variety is definitely the spice of life! Later, after a first-class dinner, I was taken, along with other guests, on an evening animal drive around the grounds. With the aid of the guide's flashlight we spotted a "*baba*" (very small alligator), some colorful "*loros*" (parrots), some very big mice, and a tree full of beautiful red and white ibis which took flight when we shined the light on them. I was sorry we had disturbed the birds, but it was a beautiful sight and they were probably used to this nightly event. I was glad to see that they returned to their tree as soon we continued down the road. I thoroughly enjoyed my stay at this upscale "dude ranch." The hot weather made the swimming pool a real treat. It was great to loll around in the water and watch tropical birds fly in and out of the open area. On my last morning at the *Dona Barbara*, I breakfasted poolside with a toucan peering over my shoulder. I was hoping nothing on my plate would catch its attention. Before leaving the area we went canoeing on a nearby lagoon and saw more "*babas*" plus herons and ibis and other aquatic inhabitants as well as some pecaris (similar to pigs) and even a tapir (usually not seen) in this area. Then it was back to Caracas—on good paved roads for which I was thankful!

My last adventure in the country was a visit to the Los Roques Archepelago—just off the coast of Venezuela—for some snorkeling. The islands are just a short hop away by plane. I will say that I have experienced better snorkeling in Hawaii, but the setting couldn't be beat. I had a room overlooking the beautiful Caribbean Sea, and each day of my visit was transported by a small boat to a different spot for my snorkeling and swimming pleasure. I was dropped off and left there for several hours with a towel, beach chair, umbrella and a cooler with lunch and drinks. The boat later returned to take me back to the hotel for happy hour and din din—very civilized!

Venezuela II

An unplanned second visit to the country took place about seven months later During my previous visit I had hoped to visit Angel Falls in Canaima National Park—the world's highest falls at 3,212 feet. It was the dry season, however, when the falls are greatly reduced. Consequently, this meant a return in the wet season to view the cascade when it comes surging down from a flat-top mesa (called a *tepui*) in a thundering torrent. This time I was accompanied by two good friends, Mark and Rick, from my L.A. running club. Once again Bill and Carol offered their hospitality in Caracas, and Bill joined us on this venture as he had never been to Angel Falls (Carol had to work). The falls were discovered in 1937 by American adventurer, Jimmie Angel when his plane got stuck in the soft mud of the mesa above the falls—it has nothing to do with "angels!" We first viewed them from the seat of a small plane. This was stunning, if a little scary, flying so close to the torrent. The following day we boarded a motorized dugout canoe and traveled upriver to a camp where we could view the falls from below. The camp itself was an experience, including a candle-lit outhouse! And our food was strictly fresh—caught daily. We slept in hammocks which at first I thought would be great fun—not so much for a stomach sleeper! From the camp we hiked a short distance to the base of the falls. I will never forget standing there and gazing up at this 3,200-foot drop.

Our final adventure on this trip was to ascend the Roraima Tepui. A *tepui* is a steep-sided flat-toped mountain, and Roraima, at 9,300 feet, is South America's highest. It was the inspiration for Sir Arthur Conan Doyle's novel "The Lost World." We began our trek in the village of Paratepui and made our way across a long stretch of open savanna (*la gran sabana*), with several hills interspersed. After three or four hours we reached our first campsite at the Rio Tek. This river can normally be crossed by wading but can rise rapidly if there are unexpected rains upstream (which we encountered on our return trip). The next day was a four-hour, mostly uphill, hike to "base camp" at the foot of the *tepui*. Looking out over the savanna from base camp at twilight was awesome (in the true sense of the word!). Day three was the real challenge. This was a 3,000-foot ascent starting out through jungle-covered slopes below Roraima's steep cliffs. Eventually the jungle began to thin and views of the savanna opened up again behind us. Shortly before reaching the top the trail became "boulder alley" where my trekking pole was a hindrance (in fact I asked a guide to carry it for me in this section doing better with my arms and legs). Good hand and footholds were essential—and not all that easy to attain at times. At last—the top! It was like nothing I had ever seen. A moonscape would be my closest description. It was very rocky and covered with craters of various sizes, some of which were filled with water. These pools were surrounded by exotic and bizarre vegetation—a number of plants which are found only on the *tepuis*. As for fauna, there was very little. The most visible creature was a small black frog, about the size of a thumbnail. It was so primitive that it neither hopped nor swam. Consequently, it was easy to photograph! Our sleeping accommodations were on a ledge underneath a rocky overhang which provided some protection from the elements. We set up our tents and called it home for two days. Our kitchen was set up on an adjacent ledge. Toilet facilities were catch as catch can, but we managed. And I'm happy to say that the "pack it in, pack it out" rule applied as far as paper goes. Our trek back down was uneventful except for the river crossing I mentioned earlier. Rain had swollen the river since our previous crossing and it was not now possible to wade across. My male companions striped off their shirts and dove in. I was not similarly inclined. Fortunately, there was a rowboat available for folks like me (and our gear). Two days later we were at the Caracas Airport heading back to L.A.

Hey world, here I am!, Los Angeles, 1939

Grammar school graduation, Los Angeles, 1948
(2nd row, 3rd from right)

With Xian Warriors, China, 2000

Tasmanian family I boarded with while picking apples, 1970
(2nd row, far right)

Irish countryside, 2007

Irish mailbox, 2007

On climb to Mt. Whitney, 2006

Local transport on Santorini, Italy, 1980s

Cheesecake pose, Los Angeles, 1980s

After New York City Marathon, 1986

With George Takei (Mr. Sulu) and fellow actor in London, 1980s

With London Hash House Harriers, 1980s

Atop Mt. Kilimanjaro, Tanzania, 1997

Jane Dods

Slight impediment on Pacific Crest Trail, 2000

Flying over the Tibetan Plateau, 2000

Flying over the Tibetan Plateau, 2000

Cute little Tibetans, 2000

Panda Sanctuary, Chendu, China, 2000

Medal stash at Gay Games, Sydney Australia, 2002

Pacific Crest Trail in So. California desert, 2002

Along the Pacific Crest Trail - water bottles left by "trail angels", 2002

Jane Dods

Warning sign along the Pacific Crest Trail in So. California desert, 2002

Along the Pacific Crest Trail - my "home away from home," 1990s

Interacting with the local fauna, Los Llanos, Venezuela, 2004

Along the Pacific Crest Trail - unexpected snow to cross in July, 2004

Two-level outhouse (for summer and winter) along the Pacific Crest Trail, 2005

Vietnamese "necklace". 2006

Sightseeing in Saigon, 2006

With friend Jan at Angor Wat 10K in Cambodia, 2006

Just prior to dawn start of 10K, Cambodia -
Angor Wat temple in background, 2006

Arctic Ocean (very windy, very cold!)

Dipping toes in Arctic Ocean, 2011

Traveling above Arctic Circle, 2011

Helping Bhutanese women build a house, 2012

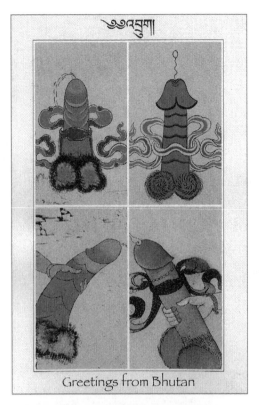

Bhutanese phallic art, 2012

For heaven's sake - is nothing sacred? - McDonalds, Lourdes, 2012

JANE WITHOUT TARZAN 89

With French friend Philippe, taking refreshment at café in Lourdes (not McDonalds!), 2012

End of Camino de Santiago at Finisterre (end of the earth), Atlantic Ocean, 2012

Fellow peregrino (pilgrim) with whom I shared an octopus dinner along the Camino de Santiago, 2012

Camino de Santiago directional sign through city in Spain, 2012

Directional sign in city outskirts, 2012

Free wine along Camino for peregrinos (pilgrims) - cheers!, 2012

At the start of Camino de Santiago, St. Jean Pied-de-Port, France, 2012

With fellow Eugene hiking buddy, Frank -
cerveza break along the Camino, 2013

Autoroute of the Camino, 2012

08/19/2006

Atop Mt. Whitney, 2006

Jane Dods

Hiking in the Pyrenees, 2012

Visit to Eugene's Sister City, Kakagawa, Japan, 1998 (Left)

Showing Kiwi heritage after trip to New Zealand, 2000 (Right)

CHAPTER 16

CENTRAL AMERICA

Belize and Guatemala
(Spelunking, Rapelling and Snorkeling)

IN DECEMBER, 2013, I JOINED ROAD SCHOLARS ONCE MORE. This time for a trip to Central America. On the way down I experienced something I had never experienced before. I was offered "priority boarding" with use of a wheelchair if I needed it (time marches on!). Little did they know that I would soon be caving, rapelling and snorkeling! I didn't need this extra service, but took it anyway so as to have my choice of space in the overhead bins. My flight pattern was Eugene/Miami/Belize. At the Belize airport I met up with five other "scholars," and we soon hopped into a van and headed for our hotel—the very plush Radisson—not my favorite type of accommodation but, hey, who's complaining (it's paid for!). My room on the sixth floor had a lovely view of the Caribbean Sea. I was supposed to have a roommate, but so far no one had appeared. After stashing my stuff and taking a shower I went down to the pool and ordered a "Belikin"—the local (and only) beer available in Belize. This is not a wine country. Then at 6:30 the group met for dinner and an introductory meeting. It was here I learned that I *did*, indeed, have a roommate. "Dixie" had just arrived a bit later. She turned out to be quite compatible, and we got along well.

One of the highlights of this trip was to view Mayan ruins. Our first such visit entailed a very pleasant 2-hour boat ride to

Lamanai—one of the largest and most excavated sites in northern Belize. I was very impressed at the lack of commercialism—only a small gift shop at the entrance.

Our main ruins-watching took place at Tikal in Guatemala. This site has over 4,000 structures with more still being excavated. It was amazing to walk through these vestiges of Mayan culture. Most of the temples had steps on the outside if one wished to climb to the top. The steepness of most of them and lack of handrails precluded this activity for me. I was quite content to view these wonders from ground level. Before returning to Belize we made a visit to Ixpanpjul Natural Park with its gorgeous nature trails and a series of suspension bridges across which we happily perambulated. As we crossed some of the bridges we were sometimes "serenaded" by howler monkeys who lived in the adjacent trees. This was NOT a soothing sound!

The two most memorable days of this trip were when we went spelunking (caving) and rappelling. These are two of the few adventurous things I had not yet tried and were major "come-ons" for my taking this trip. The cave, we were told, held many Mayan ceremonial artifacts and burial chambers—certainly piquing one's curiosity. After driving on a series of bad roads we arrived at the start of this venture. Here we were issued a hard hat and a miner's light. We then took off on a jungle path, soon coming to the first of three rivers we had to cross before reaching the cave. It was maybe 100 feet across with a very rocky bottom. Even with my walking stick I found the footing very uneven and needed to take the hand of a guide to maintain my stability. Eventually, after two more similar river crossings we reached the opening of the cave through which a river flowed. We started off by walking but soon were "swimming" (dog paddling) as the water gradually got deeper. (I reflect at this time on the May, 2018, cave rescue in Thailand. It's probably good that hadn't yet happened or I may not have gone on this trip.) At times we had to squeeze through very narrow openings. Other times we had to climb up very steep and rocky passages. The scenery along the way, in the light of our headlamps, was "unreal"—stalactites, stalagmites, a variety of ancient utensils and artifacts embedded in the rock, along with ancient bones were visible from time to time. After an hour or so we reached the end of our watery trek—a very large opening containing even more artifacts and bones as well as the almost intact skeleton of a (presumably) young girl dating back to approximately 900 AD. When we turned around to go back I felt as if I couldn't possibly repeat what I had just gone through, but there was no other choice unless I wanted to become a 2013 AD skeleton for folks to come across in years to come! At least on the way back there were no surprises. When we emerged from the cave and re-crossed the rivers we, very gratefully, reached the van and the dry clothes we had brought along. A steaming hot bath that evening was immensely enjoyable!

My other "most memorable" event was rappelling. This entailed first hiking uphill for about an hour. Rusty railings lined this trail which definitely made the going easier for me. The hike ended at the top of a cliff. Here we were issued a harness and helmet and given instructions for the descent. We then lined up to make the drop. I must say I was a tad nervous, especially after witnessing the young girl ahead of me who got cold feet saying, "I can't do this!" as she got to the edge of the cliff. I steeled myself to be brave and made it a point to not look down as I backed off the top. We were tethered, but it was still a frightening experience. We had to kick our way about ten feet down the rocky face. At that point we were hanging free with our legs dangling from the harness. We were now able to control our descent by pulling on a rope. Once I felt in control, I was able to enjoy the experience and looked down upon the canopy of trees beneath me. This is an experience, while thrilling, I will probably not repeat.

Our last activity before returning home was a good deal less adrenalin-inducing—several days at the Jaguar Reef Lodge on the Caribbean for some snorkeling. Dixie and I had a lovely room facing the water with our own little veranda (where I could sip my

Biliken's). I must say that I have experienced better snorkeling in other parts of the world, but it was enjoyable nevertheless. Getting out to the reef in the choppy water was a 45-minute adventure in itself. Once there, however, the water was reasonably calm and we put on our masks and fins and went for a look. Unfortunately, my mask got a big foggy, but one of the guides gave me some de-fogger which cleared things up. The coral formations were quite interesting. The lack of fish, however, disappointing. Before heading back to shore we stopped at a nearby Smithsonian marine research center and were given an interesting tour, explaining what this important station does.

On our last day we were given the option of more snorkeling, but both Dixie and I decided to stay ashore. I took advantage of the free kayaks on the beach outside our room and went for a pleasant paddle followed by a leisurely swim. Great way to wind up this Central American sojourn.

— CHAPTER 17 —

AFRICA

Morocco, North Africa

My first steps on the Dark Continent took place in the 1980's. Three friends and I flew to Madrid where we rented a car and had a grand time exploring Spain as well as Portugal. Then, as we were driving along the *Costa del Sol* (and the Strait of Gibraltar) we suddenly realized that Africa was just across the water, so why not have a look at a new continent? We put our car and ourselves on a ferry, sailed by Prudential's well-known rock, Gibraltar, and before long landed in the town of Tangier on the coast of Morocco. It was quite a thrill to step off the boat and realize we were in Africa! Before long, however, we realized that we had a problem. Because we had a car, we were considered "rich." Each time we stopped the car we were swarmed by (mostly) young boys who wanted to take us to a hotel, to a restaurant to a "tourist" spot, etc. And they usually attempted to "wash" the windows with dirty rags. This was really, really annoying. We realized that this was part of the culture and that these boys could probably well use whatever tips they were given, but it was not something that we were willing to deal with on a daily basis. So instead of driving some 400 miles south to Marrakech as we had planned, we made it about 125 miles to Fes where we stayed in a Holiday Inn and enjoyed Bloody Marys (a Muslim no-no) by the swimming pool while we decided what to do next. This is definitely NOT something I would ordinarily do in a foreign country. Normally, I want to soak in the culture and stay at a 2-star hotel or a hostel, but this intrusion of our privacy was just too much. The next day, however, we did hire "Abdul" (seems like all the boys are named Abdul) to show us around the local "souk" (old marketplace). This would have been impossible without a guide. The streets are little more than alleyways and wind every which way. We would have been lost in minutes on our own. It was fascinating to see the locals and the wares they displayed—things you definitely don't see at Wal-Mart! Abdul took us to a couple of shops that I'm sure were run by friends of his, but that was O.K. We each bought something to remind us of the unique experience. I found a lovely little brass (I think) tea pot.

Durban, South Africa—World Masters Games

I'VE ALREADY TALKED ABOUT MY LOVE OF RUNNING, AND NOW I will describe another international event I was fortunate to take part in. Every two years the World Association of Masters Athletes (WAMA) puts on a championship track meet in a different part of the world. These meets showcase the *creme de la creme* of masters track and field athletes where the competition is broken down into five year age-groups. Women are eligible to compete at 35 and men at 40. The oldest group is usually contested in the 100-104 age-division. There are no qualifying times or distances. Any athletes who wish to attend and rub shoulders with their amazing contemporaries are welcome to participate. In 1997 the championships were held in Durban, South Africa. This sounded way too exotic for me to miss, so plans were made with my travel agent and in July I took off. At 62, I competed in the 60-64 age-group and was curious to see what my international competition might be. I was in no way a gold-medal contender, but not too shabby either. The journey from Eugene to Durban is a L-O-N-G one. It entailed flights from Eugene to New York, then on to Johannesburg via South African Airlines, and finally a jumper flight over to Durban, on the Indian Ocean. This city is a resort town and somewhat resembles Coney

Island with its beachfront hotels and touristy restaurants. I was glad to find that my hotel was not in this section but directly across the street from the gorgeous city hall and a lovely park which featured the ornate Vasco da Gama clock (a landmark in town). An efficient shuttle system picked up athletes from their lodgings throughout the city and transported them to the competition venues each day. It was great to run into some familiar faces from the U.S. when I picked up my credentials and later at various events. I had registered for three events—the 5,000 meter run, the long jump, and the 10,000-meter cross-country team relay. As expected, I did not medal in the 5,000 or the long jump, but did manage a silver in the cross country team relay event along with my U.S.A. teammates, Eve and Mary. It was, indeed, a thrill to stand on the podium and have the medals put around our necks. Before leaving the area I partook in a spirited run with the Durban Hash House Harriers—a chapter of a world-wide organization whose members are sometimes known as "drinkers with a running problem." A member goes out and marks a course (usually 10K) with flour—the weirder the better—over fences, through waterways (if possible) and through as much "shiggy" (unpleasant vegetation) as possible. All the while yelling "On On" when a spot of flour is spotted. A crazy bunch, indeed! Then on to experience some other parts of the continent.

Kingdom of Lesotho, Cape Town and the Cape of Good Hope

BEFORE HOPPING DOWN TO CAPE TOWN I DECIDED TO HAVE a look at Lesotho—Africa's land-locked kingdom in the mountains. Its distinction is having the highest low point of any country in the world (some 4,500 ft.). Getting there was an adventure in itself. The road was absolutely the worst I had ever encountered in all of my travels (as I mentioned before). It was, of course, unpaved, rutted and very curvy. Remnants of vehicles that hadn't made it were visible from time to time. The vehicle we rode in had ample hand-holds for its four passengers to help keep us from landing in each other's laps as we rocked and rolled up the road. When we dared, we stole glances at the stark, mountainous landscape outside. Every now and then some greenery and a creek would appear. Eventually we reached Sani Pass (8,700 ft) and had a beer at the Sani Top Chalet—Africa's highest pub—the Hash House Harriers would love it here!

My next stop was the lovely city of Cape Town. One of the athletes in Durban had given me the name of a wonderful guest house where I procured a room for about $25 overlooking Table Bay—Cape Town's gorgeous harbor. Great location, great price! Behind me loomed Table Mountain, South Africa's iconic flat-topped landmark. When it's cloudy the locals say the mountain has on a tablecloth. Time constraints did not allow me to climb to the top, but it was a grand sight to behold from below. During my brief stay I ambled along the Victoria and Albert Waterfront overlooking the beautiful bay and strolled through Bo-Kap—the very colorful Muslim neighborhood where the houses are painted in vibrant colors such as turquoise-blue and lavender.

Next on the agenda was a tour to the Cape of Good Hope and surrounding area. Having stood at the tip of South America at Cape Horn, it was fitting and proper that I should now stand at the rocky tip of Africa. The drive down the cape was gorgeous. We had a bit of a baboon attack before we arrived. The primates in this area are very aggressive and think nothing of jumping on (or in) your vehicle as you pass through. Fortunately, we escaped such intrusion, but the car in front of us had left a rear window open and got unexpected company. Shrieks were heard from both humans and ape! After soaking in the ambience at the cape, we headed back towards Durban along the Indian Ocean, making a stop at the Jackass Penguin Colony on the beach at Simon's Town. This is one of two mainland colonies of these endearing birds which are found only in Southern African waters. It was delightful to watch them waddle about in this natural habitat. Next on the agenda was a long flight to Nairobi.

Mt. Kilimanjaro, Nairobi, and the Masai Mara

IN THE PROLOGUE TO THIS BOOK, I MENTIONED BEING ON THE slopes of Mt. Kilimanjaro. I shall now elaborate on how I got there. As I was perusing the map of Africa prior to my trip to Durban my eyes landed on "Mt. Kilimanjaro"—hmmm. Well, as long as I would be on the same continent, why not, so I started making plans for the trek. Kili is not a technical climb (no ropes or pitons), but it is an arduous 5-day or more up and down venture. Through my association with the local Hash House Harriers in Eugene, I was given the name of a Hasher who was a travel agent in Nairobi—perfect! He made all the necessary arrangement for me. First was a look at the city of Nairobi. He booked, at my request, a cheap ($25.00) room in town. I arrived after dark and was let out at a building with an open-air entrance. I soon found out what it felt like to be a minority. There was nothing but a sea of black faces around me. This was fine, this was Africa, but it did make me feel a bit out of place. I went up to my room which was also fine (if modest), put my stuff down and decided to go out for a bite to eat. On passing the desk I asked the clerk if he could recommend anything. He suggested I not go out. Oh my! I returned to my room and scarfed down a bit of leftover airline food I had in my bag. The next morning I called the travel agent and requested an upgrade. I then walked to his office downtown which was only about a mile away. I soon found out that while downtown Nairobi is a modern, first-world city, its outskirts soon revert to third-world conditions. Normally, I prefer to stay in simple, local lodgings, but when safety is an issue I make exceptions. After meeting with my Hasher travel guy I was transported to a 4-star hotel with a swimming pool (I was glad that I had brought along my bathing suit). I spent two nights here before departing for Tanzania and Kili. A visit to the local market was most interesting—particularly the display of offal—odd organ meats (none of which I wished to put in my shopping bag). The best thing about the city is that it encompasses Nairobi National Park—the only game reserve within a major city. I had a wonderful time strolling through the environs of this urban park and admiring its inhabitants. Before leaving Nairobi I joined the local Hashers for a romp. We started at the pool deck of another 4-star hotel, then dashed downstairs through the lobby and out into the street. Before long we found ourselves in the before-mentioned "third-world" conditions. It was quite an eye-opener and quite fascinating. After about an hour we ran back up to the pool deck and enjoyed our beer and spirited foolishness.

Then it was on to Tanzania and Kili. I boarded a bus in Nairobi and six hours later arrived in Arusha in northeast Tanzania. Here I was met by a local tour guide and taken to a hotel to spend the night before heading out the next morning on the trek. This town is a major staging point for folks attempting the climb. In Nairobi, I had paid for a "package deal" which included hotel accommodations in Arusha before and after the climb. This hotel consisted of a number of attractive bungalows dotting the property which were quite comfortable (with modern amenities). That evening, after an excellent dinner, I was visited in my room by my climbing guide. He was there to make sure I had everything necessary for the next five days. Not that I had to carry much—only a day pack. The porters would carry everything else as well as food and cooking paraphernalia (not light!). I had hoped to join a group on this venture so as to share the cost of the guide and porters, but there was no one else booked to go at the same time I had planned. So it was just me and my entourage—a guide and three porters. I had never been so attended before. It felt a little strange. I had been advised not to book a cut-rate outfit as the guides sometimes push their clients too fast so they can't make it to the top. Of course if that happens the guides don't have to go to the top either! Well, this certainly wasn't the case with my guys. The operative words were *pole, pole* (Swahili for slowly, slowly). I was actually held back a bit by this pace, particularly on summit day, but it paid great dividends.

After a good night's rest, we set out the following morning on the Marangu Route—probably the most popular of several routes to Uhuru (the top). We would ascend approximately 3,000 feet a day, with a final climb very early on the fourth day of approximately 4,000 feet to the top. The route starts out at approximately 6,000 feet in a rain forest. The going is easy and the verdant scenery very nice. The exciting part was to realize that I was finally on the slopes of Kilimanjaro. As we hiked, we came across a number of other parties, and it was always fun to chat and learn where everyone was from. At the end of each day this route offers trekkers small A-frame huts in which to bed down (the only route to do so). "Bed" is not really the operative word, as the sleeping accommodations consisted of 4-6 mattresses on the floor on which we placed our sleeping bags. You simply open a door, see if there's a vacant mattress, ask one of the porters for your sleeping bag and stake your claim. If you're wondering about sanitation, it was quite basic—a pit toilet of some sort (90% of the time) and a bucket of hot water in the morning and evening (100% of the time). Dinner was served in the dining hut—a fairly large area with a number of tables set up. Each climbing party had its own distinctive place mats, so you always knew your place. The porters cooked outside over a fire and brought in each course as it was ready (there were several). Everything was quite tasty—better than I eat at home (but that's not saying much!). I was advised that if I hired a cut-rate outfit I was likely to be served potatoes and cabbage three times a day. The second day led us out of the rain forest onto "moor-like" terrain with some distant views. One of my favorite photos was taken this day just after I exited an outhouse (one of the few along the route). The outhouse door partially framed the "snows of Kilimanjaro" in the distance. The best view I've ever had from a public restroom! Again, the walking was easy, Although we climbed from 9,000 to 12,000 feet, the ascent was gradual and the trail well-maintained. We passed sparsely-vegetated high-desert terrain with several exotic African blooms which I didn't recognize. Day's end found us again at our

A-frame huts. We once more staked claim to a mattress, enjoyed an excellent meal and conversation with a couple of other climbing parties. Then early to bed in preparation for our penultimate day before the summit attempt.

So far the weather had been ideal. I was clad in shorts and a T-shirt and carried a light jacket in my pack for the afternoon. Day three, from 12,000 to 15,000 feet, definitely brought a temperature change. Time for long pants and a heavier jacket. On this day we got views of Kili's three volcanic cones—Kibo, Mawenzi. and Shira—again passing through unique flora on our way to Kibo Hut—our destination for the day. This is a stone hut with a couple of rooms that sleep 10-15 people in bunk beds. After saturating ourselves with the fantastic views, we went back inside at dusk for a light dinner and shortly thereafter to our bunks. Sleep, however, was elusive. The prospect of tomorrow's venture totally took over my mind. Well, I didn't have much time to dwell on it as we were awakened about 12:30 a.m. to get ready. It is essential to get up and down within a certain time frame. My wardrobe had now changed dramatically from the previous days. At this elevation of 15,520 feet, in the middle of the night, it was about 15 degrees. I had brought along my ski wear (including hand and foot warmers). My guide, Soster, and I began the ascent about 1 a.m. (the porters stayed behind). He went out at such a slow pace that I had to hold back a bit to keep my nose out of his jacket. A line of climbers snaked up ahead of us. Looking up at the sinuous glow of their headlamps was an amazing sight. Then, lo and behold, we passed someone, and then several more as we plodded along *pole, pole*. And then about three hours into the climb a couple of people turned around and came back down towards us, unable to continue (very likely because of ascending too quickly or altitude sickness). When I next looked at my watch it was 4:30 a.m. The going was getting steeper and the soil of the trail was becoming a loose scree, making each step quite arduous. I began to think, "What have I gotten myself into?" I wasn't dying, however, so on I trudged. About 6:00 a.m., just after sunrise, we reached Gilman's Point at 16,685 feet (the first summit). The views from here are stupendous—looking out on the plains of Africa. Many folks consider this their goal and head back down from here. Not me. I was determined to get to Uhuru Peak, the true summit. My guide checked me out, considered me fit, and on we went. It was another 2 hours and 2,600 feet to the top. Now we were walking on hard-packed snow—much easier than the scree. Unfortunately, about half way there I had a desperate need to find a toilet—ha, ha, ha! There was nothing to do but step behind the largest rock I could find and pull down my pants, shielded from my guide as best as I could. Just as I squatted, however, a party who had already been to the top came around a curve and got a full view of the proceedings. Oh well, that's life in the raw. Hopefully it was too cold to take pictures! Finally, at 8:30 a.m. we stood on "the roof of Africa" as designated by a sign—what a feeling! After Soster took my picture holding the sign, he pulled out of his pack a thermos of hot tea and a container of English "biscuits" (cookies). We didn't tarry long as we had a long, long hike back downhill to our hut for the night. When we got back to Gillman's Point and the scree, some of the younger climbers hopped, skipped, and jumped their way downhill. Not me. I sustained a stately pace for the next four hours to our hut for the night. It was now 3:30 p.m. We had been on the go for about fifteen hours, and I was absolutely beat! I went directly to a hut, closed the door and said not to disturb me until the next morning—not even for dinner (I had some snacks with me). The following morning we descended to the trailhead. My entourage and I then returned to my hotel where I treated them to beers in the garden—a local custom which I was happy to oblige. One of the bottles (minus the beer) is now sitting on a cabinet in my living room!

My last adventure in Africa was a safari to see the Big 5 (lions, rhinos, leopards, elephants, and cape buffalo)—strictly photo-graphic! This took place in the Masai Mara region. I opted for a low-cost outfit since the animal-viewing options seemed to be pretty much the same—whatever you paid. Perhaps I wouldn't be able to view them at night from a bed in my first class tent with a drink in my hand, but the daytime viewing was pretty much "equal opportunity." Whatever guide spotted an animal, he would get in touch with the other guides in the area and let them know. One of my favorite spottings was a leopard lounging in a tree looking like a big pussy cat with its paws dangling over the limb. I was happy to return to my vintage canvas pup tent at the end of the day, rest a bit, and then get in line for a delicious dinner (served buffet-style). Since there was no hot water available at the camp the plastic plates were always a little greasy, but who cares! The Masai stood tall in their colorful garb. One of them spotted my (very cheap) Casio watch and pointed to my wrist. He seemed to be very taken by it, so we struck a deal. I traded it for a terrific beaded bracelet he wore—not to be duplicated! I did wonder, however, what he would do when the battery died.

— CHAPTER 18 —

ASIA

Japan I

I HAVE VISITED JAPAN TWICE. THE FIRST TIME WAS IN THE 70s to join my vagabond friend Art who was doing the hippie thing, traveling across Europe and Asia (at a somewhat advanced age!). I was accompanied by three friends from L.A., Jerry, Joe and Willie. When Art met us in Tokyo we almost didn't recognize him with his long hair and beard. He had played the part to the hilt. The dysentery in India, however, provided a little more realism than he would have liked and put him in a local hospital for a couple weeks before meeting us. He had lost some weight, but otherwise seemed to be in pretty good shape after his nearly year-long odyssey. While we were in Tokyo, we were very fortunate to visit the apartment of two local people. Art had met the husband, then a student, some years earlier when he was traveling in the U.S. and was invited to visit him if he ever got to Tokyo. Well, here we were—all four of us! Yoshi now had a wife, and space is at absolute premium in Tokyo. There was a living room, a bedroom, a bathroom, and the "tatami" room—the only uncluttered space in the apartment—furnished with tatami mats and a kind of altar. That's where we slept. We didn't see the bedroom, but the furniture in the living room was placed side by side for lack of space. The kitchen was basically the size of a closet where you could stand in one place and take care of all the chores. On the other hand, the bathroom held a big tub (a cultural must). Yoshi and his wife were most gracious hosts, and we were delighted to experience their hospitality.

Being a "bath person" I had to go to one of the public baths for this experience. You wash yourself while squatting down by a little faucet at the side of the pool. When clean, you immerse yourself (very slowly) into the steaming hot water and soak. Even for one who loves hot water, this was almost too much for me. I didn't soak for long!

We stayed in Tokyo and environs for about ten days. A highlight was a very early morning (4 a.m) visit to the fish market with my friend Willie (she was the only one willing to get up so early). Somehow we managed to find our way to the waterfront and watched with amazement the frantic activity of fish and man. Actually, two young-ish Western females seemed to be just as much of an attraction to the workers as *they* were to us—lots of pointing and smiling! Another unusual tourist stop was the Penis Shrine. I guess these organs are revered in Japan. I had my photo rather irreverently taken astride one the exhibits just for fun. Before leaving the country, I was the only one of our group to climb Mt. Fuji—but then you might have guessed that! It was a grand experience. I made my way up slowly with people of all ages, and I mean ALL ages (a number over 80—which I am now!). I bought a walking stick which was branded at various "stations" on the way up (it now hangs in my condo). Experiencing sunrise from the top supposedly gives one good luck for the rest of one's life, and so far this seems to be working.

Japan II

THE SECOND VISIT TOOK PLACE SOME TWENTY-FIVE YEARS later (in 1998) after I had moved to Eugene. One of Eugene's sister cities is Kakagawa, Japan. Eugene is a running town, and Japan is a running-oriented country which puts on the Kakagawa Marathon. This is an annual event to which top runners from Eugene are invited and given all the perks one might expect afforded an invitee.

I was not one. However, ordinary runners, like myself, could take part in an accompanying 10K. Our expenses were not paid, but we did get to home-stay with a Japanese family. That gave us a terrific opportunity to experience ordinary life in another culture. I wasn't crazy about the raw fish for breakfast, but I downed it with a smile. Not hard to do when surrounded by my wonderful new family. On leaving, our hosts presented my American roommate and me with happi coats (a kind of a short kimono)—a super going-away present. The 10K was also a very interesting experience. It's always exciting to run in different countries and not know what's around the next bend.

I expanded the official trip for a few days on my own. Most stirring was a visit to the Hiroshima Peace Memorial Museum which housed many sobering sights of this dark chapter in our history. On the grounds outside, there is a paper crane memorial to a young a-bomb victim. She thought if she could make 1,000 cranes she would survive (she got to 664). Children now make cranes to display at this site.

Next on my agenda was a visit to Nagano, site of the 1998 Winter Olympics held earlier that year. My nephew worked for CBS at the time and was a member of their production team. It was a very quick visit. Leaving the train station and stepping out into the city I immediately became illiterate. I could read nothing. It's quite different in Europe and other parts of the world where you, at least, share a common alphabet. I wandered along the main drag for a couple of hours, had a cup of tea when I spotted others doing same through a window, and then headed back to the station. From there I traveled about an hour north to a delightful hot springs area. Just as I got off the train, I was "picked up" by a young local woman who approached me and asked if I needed any help. She recognized me as an American and wanted to practice her English (she would be studying at Tokyo University the following year to become an English teacher). Of course I needed some help—I had never been here before! Consequently, she walked me to the local hostel and said she would come by the next morning to show me around. After securing my bunk in the "women's room" I headed out to an adjacent bathhouse. I first entered the "disrobing room" which led to the "hot pool room." Before entering the pool, however, I was careful to observe the protocol I had learned in Tokyo—scrub on the sidelines first. The pool is strictly for soaking. Getting in was another experience. The water was so hot I could barely tolerate it. I could only stand it for about 3 minutes at a time—hoisting myself to the edge of the pool between dips. The following morning "Sachimi," indeed, appeared at the hostel and took me for a tour of her home town—a delightful experience. She definitely got in a great deal of English-speaking experience as she showed me around, and I had the pleasure of her company.

On my last day in Japan, while waiting for the train to the airport, I got to talking with a guy on the platform. He was a Dane who had married a Japanese woman, and they were visiting her relatives. While she chatted away with her family, he and I chatted away (Scandinavians always speak English). In the course of the conversation, I mentioned that I had never been to Denmark. He then whipped out a card which he handed to me and said I was welcome to stay at his home anytime. The following year he picked me up in Copenhagen railway station for a visit. That's sort of how my life goes.

China I

CHINA HAS SEEN ME ON ITS SHORES TWICE. THE FIRST TIME was in 1982. I had spotted an ad in the *L.A. Times* stating "Hike the Great Wall of China"—again, how could I resist? Upon further inquiry I learned that the tour operators consisted of only two people. I was so taken with the idea, however, that I didn't do much checking and signed up immediately. It turned out that only myself and one other intrepid soul (a guy in his 50s) made up the group. All

I can say is that it was a good thing this guy and I were experienced hikers/backpackers. The two "leaders" knew how to arrange a trip but very little about hiking and backpacking. My travel buddy and I wound up giving *them* advice! Arriving in Beijing after dark (after God knows how many hours) we were whisked to our hotel and shown to our rooms where we immediately tucked in for the night. The next morning when I drew back the drapes I saw a sea of traffic on the street below—(almost) all bicycles! As I said, this was 1982 and there was no private ownership of cars in China. They were reserved for military, diplomatic and governmental personnel. Well, be it L.A. or Beijing, I needed to go out for my morning run. I tried to stay as far as possible to the right so as not to impede traffic, but every head turned as they passed me by. I doubt if they had ever seen a Western woman joining them on their morning commute. After a while I turned off the main road and found myself in a non-20th century neighborhood enclave. Here there were simple one-story dwellings where the running water was from a tap outside in the street. The residents were busily washing up, brushing their teeth and shaving, etc. I was so interested in watching the proceedings that I lost my sense of direction. Never mind, my new acquaintances eventually pointed me back, with gusto and grins, to the main road. I'm certain I livened up their morning!

As I stated earlier, this trip was called "Hike the Great Wall of China." Well, it was more like hiking *in the vicinity of* the Great Wall. From Beijing we took the train north to Harbin—known as Manchuria in earlier times. Here I experienced another bit of culture shock. Needing to use the restroom I was directed to the rear of the station where one simply walked behind a wall and squatted, or whatever. Carrying TP was a MUST! Harbin was a very interesting city. Being in the far north of the country it experiences wicked winters. People's wood piles were usually higher than the roofs of their homes. This wood was their life-line in the winter. In their bedrooms, they slept warmly atop platforms under which a fire burned all night—obviously, proper fireproofing was a major concern!

The next day we went to the CITS (Chinese International Travel Service) office and met our local hiking guides. At that time independent hiking groups were not allowed in the country so several of the CITS folks had to accompany us. They could not imagine why people would pay a great deal money to travel somewhere only to carry their belongings on their backs. They wanted to transport our packs by vehicle each day. We finally managed to convince them that we really *did* want to carry our packs. They reluctantly let us have our way. What we did need their help for, however, was showing us where the trails were in the vicinity of the Great Wall. These were, in the main, old logging roads. We camped each night in lovely forested areas. I remember one night, specifically, when we no sooner had gotten our tents up than the heavens opened up. Fortunately, my tent didn't leak. After making my dinner I lay back thinking, "I'm on a Chinese hillside in a rainstorm!" The reason we couldn't hike totally atop the Wall is that it has disintegrated in many sections over its centuries-old existence. As partial compensation for our initial disappointment, we were led through villages where no one had ever seen Westerners. These locals lined the path to watch us walk by. The kids were usually the first to smile, with some of the old people slowly giving us big (if mostly toothless) grins as well. This was truly a unique experience.

For the most part, the hiking was not very strenuous. When we did get into rough terrain, however it was *really* rough. Our guides used large knives to whack at the dense vegetation allowing us to squeeze through. We were told this was tiger country, but we didn't run into anything wilder than some rabbits—disappointing! Oh, except for a mouse that chewed its way into my tent one night.

On our final night in the country we attended a performance by Chinese acrobats in Beijing. I could hardly watch two of the women contortionists whose seemingly impossible positions made me cringe!

China II

MY SECOND TRIP TO CHINA TOOK PLACE IN 2000. THIS TIME my friends Fran and Pat joined me, and we went with a well-established group—Overseas Adventure Travel. Besides being very well-organized this outfit limits its trips to just 16 people. The main draw of this particular itinerary was that it included a visit to Tibet. While in Beijing we visited the usual tourist attractions—the Forbidden City (with Mao's visage peering out over the populace), Tianamen Square, and the Temple of Heaven, with a look at the empress' stone boat as well. We also walked a short section of the Great Wall near the city with a lot of other tourists.

A few days later we hopped on an overnight train to visit the terra cotta warriors and their horses in Xian. It was wonderful to hear the clickity-clack of the rails as we went to sleep. The next morning we were off to see this incredible display which dates back to the Qin Dynasty (211-206 BC). It was unearthed in 1974 by local farmers digging in their fields and is now a world heritage site. To gaze out on these some 1,000 mute warriors was amazing. One could sense the power that lay behind their silence.

Then began a 4-day journey down the Yangtze River. We boarded our boat at the Xian dock and headed for Chongquin (formerly Chungking)—the jumping off point for Tibet. I was pleasantly surprised by my commodious cabin complete with private bath and large picture window. I later learned that this was a British ship, the *Victoria 1*. Consequently, we were given a Western breakfast. This was very much appreciated after a week or more of strictly Chinese cuisine (and grappling awkwardly with chopsticks). Not that I don't like to try foreign foods, but a steady diet gets to be a bit much. The highlight of this cruise was to view the construction area of the Three Gorges Dam. This tremendous hydro-electric project was 16 years in the making (1993-2009). At one point we got off the boat and were driven a short distance to a construction site where we were shown a model of the dam. We were then taken to an overlook where we could view the construction site itself. It was almost dusk, and the weather was quite murky creating a somewhat surreal aspect. We couldn't see details, just the movement of the workers below as they labored in the glare of electric bulbs strung about the site. Some of them seemed to be using very primitive tools (pick and shovel). There was much controversy surrounding this project as it displaced over one million people and submerged over 1,000 archeological and historic sites (not to mention familial treasures of the residents who were uprooted). As we sailed down the river we could see markings along the banks indicating the high and low water marks once the dam was completed. Another lasting memory of this cruise was lying back on my bunk and gazing out my window at the Chinese countryside as we passed slowly by. Not an inch of arable land was left bare.

On the fourth day we docked in Chongquin. What a change it was to enter this teeming city (30 million in 2015) after our slo-mo days on the Yangtze. At the time we visited it was, unfortunately, known as the foggiest (smoggiest) city in China and the river there was deplorably polluted. We didn't spend much time in Chongquin. Our main outing there was a visit to the Flying Tigers Museum. This museum honors the American WWII pilots who flew "over the hump" from India to China to help re-supply the Chinese in their struggle against Japan.

Our next trip segment was a flight to Lhasa, in Tibet. We took off in the pitch black of early morning. By the time the flight attendants began serving breakfast, however, we were treated to the pink glow of sunrise over the Tibetan Plateau—pretty amazing! As we approached the airport the land below appeared very brown and barren. There is little vegetation at 12,000 feet. Normally, altitude is not a problem for me, but as soon as we got off the plane a guy next to me lit up a cigarette which made me quite queasy. I managed the short walk to the terminal where I sat down and soon felt better. The city of Lhasa is a 2-hour drive from the airport, and by the time we got to town I felt fine. Unlike Kathmandu and other exotic cities I have visited, Lhasa has no charm. It just sits there flat on the plateau (although massive mountains are visible in the distance). It is built very practically in a grid pattern. We were taken to a 3-star hotel and shown our accommodations—which were excellent (all the modern amenities). After a short rest a few of us went for a walk in the neighborhood. One of the more interesting establishments we passed was an "oxygen shop"—handy if you suddenly run out of breath! During our walk we passed a woman sitting at a sewing machine on the sidewalk (foot-pedal treadle, of course). As my backpack had a few seams that needed strengthening, I handed it over to her to reinforce. About 10 minutes later she handed it back to me newly reinforced. Price?—about a dollar. Dinner that night was served buffet-style and included yak lung—hey, when in Tibet! We sat on benches adorned with beautiful Tibetan rugs. The best part of this meal for me, however, was sharing my bench with the "house cat" who had jumped up next to me (I surreptitiously slipped him slivers of yak lung which I was perfectly willing to share). After eating, we were treated to a little show of local song and dance. My friend Pat got up and joined them in a number! We were glad it didn't last too long, though, as there was no heat in the building, and when the sun went down it got really cold (we had been told to wear caps and gloves to dinner). Fortunately I was able to warm up in a hot bath back at the hotel.

The next day we visited a Tibetan home where we were served yak butter tea accompanied by *tsampa,* if we wished. *Tsampa* is Tibet's staple foodstuff, the staff of life of the locals for centuries. It consists mainly of moistened roasted barley flour which is formed into a kind of dough ball and dipped into one's tea. This combination wasn't bad, but I definitely prefer my morning mocha and a bagel! Later that day we experienced the highlight of our visit to Lhasa—a tour of the Potala Palace. No longer the residence of the Dalai Lama who was forced to relocate to India during the Tibetan Uprising of 1959, it is now a museum. Gazing upon this iconic structure takes one's breath away—its immensity is awesome. The entry is through a smallish door at the bottom of the massive structure. There was barely enough light inside to see where we were going—adding to the mysteriousness of the tour (we were told to bring flashlights to view details). There were great, high ceilings and lots of Buddhas and tapestries displayed. Vats of yak butter with floating wicks helped to provide illumination. On reaching the top, we stepped out through a doorway onto a rooftop where we gazed out at the panoramic view spread below us. Fortunately, the weather was sunny and clear as a bell (so unlike Chungking!). Then it was 300 steps back down again.

The next stop on the road was a visit to Chendu—the home of a giant panda breeding sanctuary. I don't need to tell you how appealing these guys were! The place was set up so you could get really close to the residents who seemed to thrive on attention. They would get in the most adorable positions while they munched on their bamboo. In addition to the giant panda, the facility also housed the lesser panda. This unusual animal resembles the cross between a raccoon and a chow dog—longish brown body, blackish legs, and a raccoon-like face plus a curly chow-like tail (when it wishes to curl it).

Finally, our last stop in China was Hong Kong. (from where we would fly home). After getting settled in our hotel a couple of us went for walk—stopping almost immediately at a McDonalds. After nearly three weeks of chowing down Asian-style, we were really ready for some American grub. A hamburger and fries never tasted so good (and no chopsticks necessary)! Bright and early the next morning Fran and I headed to Kowloon Park—she to join the locals in a group tai chi exercise session and me to get in a run. Unlike my previous running experience in China (Beijing in the 80s), I turned no heads this time as I strode through the park and environs. At one point I passed a pond filled with pink flamingos—a lovely sight—not seen as I run through Eugene! Our final day in Hong Kong we visited Aberdeen Harbor and Repulse

Bay—taking the tram up to Victoria Peak -and later boarding the iconic Star Ferry for a short ride. What an incredibly interesting city—so unlike its commie cousins!

Bangkok and Nepal

NOVEMBER OF 1996 SAW ME HEADED FOR NEPAL. ONE OF MY L.A. running buddies, Mark, visited that country a couple of times a year to pick up goods for resale in the U.S. This time he invited some of his friends to join him and go on a trek. Of course I jumped at this chance. This trip just happened to coincide with the annual grand procession of the royal barges down the Chao Phraya River in Bangkok (a stopover on the way to Kathmandu). This pageant was worth the trip in itself. Each year the river is briefly transformed into a glittering stage that has for centuries defined the Thai nation. It was especially significant the year I visited as it turned out to be the 50th anniversary of the reign of their beloved King Bhumibol Adulyadej (who passed away in 2016). The golden spires of riverside temples formed a stunning background for the 53 gilded royal barges of the royal flotilla as it glided by. The boats are long, sleek, and richly ornamented—their prows carved in the forms of mythical creatures. And they are rowed with exquisite precision. Many locals who live along the parade route sell seats on the decks of their modest riverside abodes to visitors, and I was lucky to get such a spot—just a couple of feet from the river itself. An unexpected bit of excitement occurred just the king's barge passed by. Thunder clapped and the heavens opened. All of us sitting on the deck had to squeeze inside their home and watch the finish on a small black-and-white TV. That, too, was an experience!

The next day I experienced culture of a decidedly different vein by joining the Bangkok Hash House Harriers in their weekly escapade. I was picked up by a local Hasher and driven to the start in a very marginal part of town. After a rousing welcome, "On-On" was called and we took off like a bunch of crazed monkeys. Our route became more and more marginal which, of course, only added to the fun. It was dark when we returned for the for "On-In" (after run party) and "Down-Downs" (chug-a-lugging a bottle of beer by people who had committed "hash crimes"—very loosely defined by each Hash group). Being a visitor, I was found guilty of three different offences. After a great deal of foolishness and conviviality, I was sent back to my hotel in a "tuk-tuk" (mechanized 3-wheeled taxi). I did not get up early the next morning.

Now on to Nepal. I was met at the Kathmandu Airport by my friend Mark and another friend from L.A., who had come over a few days earlier to join the trek (yet another friend joined us later). What a feeling it was to set foot on this exotic land! A taxi took us to the Icelandic View Hotel in the tourist district of Thamel. How this hotel in the middle of Asia got its name, I'll never know—sorta like Sarah Palin being able to see Russia from her house! My room was quite nice with (almost) modern plumbing—the shower tended to soak everything in the small bathroom (no curtain), but it did manage to keep one clean. The ancient city of Kathmandu is fascinating—narrow, winding streets with little shops and sidewalk vendors everywhere. The butcher cut up his wares on a board on the sidewalk outside his shop. There were also tiny shrines tucked away in niches that caught one's eye. We had a delightful time soaking in the atmosphere. Every now and then someone would come up to Mark or one of the other guys and ask if they wanted to buy some "ganja" (marijuana). I guess they looked like better prospects than a middle-aged woman in her hiking skirt. Yes, "hiking skirt." Mark said it would be a mark of respect to wear this when we visited his Nepalese friends. I went to a thrift store and bought a very nice garment for $2.00. It turned out to be perfect for the trek, as well as for social occasions, and was very practical for potty stops along the trail! We were fortunate to be in town for Dewali, the 5-day Festival of Lights. This is the major holiday of the year for Hindus. People spruce themselves and their homes up, and floral displays adorn the city. At night, lamps and candles are seen everywhere and, frequently, the sound of fireworks is heard—another forever memory.

Then on to the trek! We got on a local bus, and seven hours after leaving Kathmandu—including two primitive "comfort" stops—we reached. the city of Pokhara (Nepal's second largest). Although it is located on a beautiful lake, the city itself is quite dusty and ramshackle. It's the major starting point for trekkers doing the Annapurna Circuit. We were supposed to be met by someone to take us to our hotel, but he was a no-show. We eventually managed to get to the hotel, but when we arrived were told the rooms Mark thought he had reserved were no longer available. We had been replaced by a Buddhist convention in town. Now what? The holiday made lodging a real problem. After some frantic phone calls Mark found us a place for $9.00 a night—a real splurge—since the original hotel had been only $1.30 a night. It's O.K. to splurge at times!

After two days in Pokhara making sure we had everything we needed (especially water and TP), we headed out by bus for a 2-hour ride to the trailhead where we began our nine-day trek on the Annapurna Circuit (about half its entire length). When we got off the bus our porters loaded up. It's amazing what these small men can carry (more than half their weight of maybe 130 lbs.)—often wearing flip-flops and lighting up cigarettes at rest stops (I feel quite sure that they do not reach old age). We, on the other hand, had only our day packs to deal with. We had opted not to go the tent camping route to in order to avoid having to set up camp each night. Instead, we stayed at tea houses which were just a step up from tents—basically, wooden buildings with no insulation, running water or electricity. They offered a small room and a bed with a mattress of sorts onto which one put one's sleeping bag. The toilets (one-holers) were out the front door (usually fairly close to the building. On the positive side, it was very atmospheric to read my book by candlelight each night, and the price was definitely right—about sixty cents a night! Another benefit of staying at the tea houses was that dinner and breakfast were served (at a very reasonable added cost). If you stay overnight you are expected to purchase their meals—which are fairly good (but sometimes over-salted). This is a real convenience for trekkers. The tea houses make more money from their meals than from their rooms.

We usually hiked six to eight hours a day on pretty demanding terrain. There was essentially no level section (one day we ascended 3,000 feet on a stone staircase). The good thing, however, was that there was no vehicular traffic. All goods come in on the backs of porters. Some were nearly bent double carrying lumber. From time to time we would stop for glass a glass of "milk-tea" (the national beverage) in a village. As we rested and sipped our tea we would look out at the 25,000-ft-plus Annapurna range in the distance which paralleled our trail to the east. The weather in November was great during the day, but sometimes a bit nippy in our drafty rooms at night.

On one particular day we ended up at a "luxury" tea house—meaning that it had a toilet facility in the same building and on the same floor as the rooms. Apparently the "moma" (Nepalese dumpling) I had eaten earlier in the day did not agree with me. I made five trips down the hall that night. Managed only a couple of hours sleep and felt AWFUL the next morning. The thought of food was atrocious, but the trek must go on! Mark asked one of the porters to hang back with me at a slower pace. The porter also took my day pack so I didn't have to carry anything. Even so, it was a struggle to keep going—had to stop twice for half-hour rests. The only thing that helped me was Coca-Cola. A porter came by with a load of Cokes on his back and I decided to try one. It seemed to help, and I was able to walk a little faster. When we arrived at our destination, the Super View Lodge (which it *did* have, unlike the Icelandic View Hotel in Kathmandu), I went directly to my room until the next morning, downing another Coke for dinner which went down well. After a good night's sleep, I was almost recovered the next morning—even managing some bread and peanut butter.

Our journey north continued with its fascinating sights, such as Tibetan pony caravans passing us on the trail and other sights right out of National Geographic. As we crossed a suspension bridge over the Kali Gandaki River we saw a party of Indians in traditional garb making their way along the almost dry riverbed below—it could have been the Middle Ages! In the village of Tatopani—which means hot water—we were delighted to find two natural hot pools just steps from our tea house. What a joy it was to immerse ourselves after numerous days on the trail. The further north we went, the colder it got. Tea houses in this area had a recessed floor below the dining table which held charcoal braziers to warm us. Right after dinner I would run to my room and curl up in my sleeping bag to try and maintain some of the heat. In the morning we simply had to warm up on the trail.

Our destination in this section was Muktinath. The temple here is one of the most important pilgrimage sites in Nepal for both Buddhists and Hindus. Behind the temple is a semi-circular wall with 108 stone faucets at a height of seven feet. The faucets all have the same shape of the head of a bull and are separated by approximately one foot. Water from the ice cold Kali Gandaki River has been diverted to flow through the mouths of these bulls. Hardy pilgrims who visit the temple sometimes stand beneath each of the spouts—we did not! From Muktinath we retraced our steps south to the little airport at Jomson where we would get our flight back to Pokhara. There were high winds that day, and I had to grasp my walking stick firmly. Our lodging in Jomson boasted "laundry facilities." This entailed going out the back door of the building, passing two lamb carcasses hanging on hooks and coming across a metal drum with a plastic bucket next to it. The procedure was to fill the bucket with water and then scrub away (with your own bar of soap, of course). The dirty water was dumped down a hole in the ground and fresh water obtained from the metal drum for the "rinse cycle." The clothes were then draped on a chain-link fence to dry. I'll never complain about laundromats again! Spent one night in Jomson and then back to Pokhara. The short flight took place in a small Everest Air plane (seated 20). The views outside our windows of the Annapurna Range were superb!

The next stop on our Nepalese adventure was a 5-hour drive to Chitwan—a jungle habitat in the south of the country bordering India. We stayed at the appropriately-named "Jungle Island Resort." The roads were horrific. We had to hold on tight to keep from bouncing off the seat. About half-way there we stopped for a break at what I can only say resembled a hovel. As we sat sipping our milk tea we looked across the room at a tub of hot water filled with dead chickens waiting to be plucked by two young boys—something you would never see at Colonel Sanders! The last seven kilometers to Chitwan consisted of little more than tire tracks which ended at a river. Here we unloaded our stuff which was then loaded into a couple of rowboats. We than jumped in (or I should say boarded very carefully) and crossed the river. From there it was about a half-mile walk to the "resort." Indeed, it was a "resort" in name only, but the accommodations were adequate, and we were certainly in the right place to see jungle life. When we first arrived we observed a couple of elephants bathing in the river. Perhaps the highlight of this portion of the trip was a dawn elephant ride. We walked to the "elephant embarkation platform" where the elephant had backed into his "parking space." The four of us then climbed up a ladder of sorts and got onto the "saddle"—basically a rigid square covered in carpeting. We each took a corner and hung on the best we could. Our legs just kind of dangled, as we tried to find elephant parts on which to place them (not always successfully). We lumbered out in a heavy morning mist which made the ride seem even more exotic. During our walk, the guide tried to lure a rhino out of the brush but was unsuccessful. Another memorable event was an afternoon bird walk where numerous varieties of feathered friends were pointed out—some familiar, some not. This continued into the early evening getting us back to our lodgings in the light of a (almost) full moon—definitely a walk to remember.

My final adventure in Nepal was a trek on the Everest base camp trail. One of the guys in our group was supposed join me, but we had had some "misunderstandings" along the way and I think he just wanted to get home to clean sheets and hot showers! So it was just me and Pemba, my Nepalese guide, and a porter on this trail. We flew out of Kathmandu in a military helicopter. All the baggage was piled in the center of the craft and passengers were seated on either side of it (feet resting on top of the cargo). Since our backs were to the windows, it was difficult to look out at the magnificent scenery we were flying through. In about 45 minutes we arrived at Lukla. This mountain-side landing strip is a bit of a challenge for pilots. One flies over planes that have not made it. After landing (successfully) I waited in the "airport restaurant"—a dingy room with a few tables and chairs—while Pemba hunted up my porter. Pemba carried his own pack. Shortly thereafter we hit the Everest Base Camp Trail where we spent the next week (climbing first up and then back down to Lukla). The tea houses in this area were similar to those on the Annapurna Circuit, but colder since we were higher up. This route took us through Namche Bazaar—a major trading center along the old salt route of yore. We spent two nights in this town acclimatizing and then headed up to the monastery at Tengboche. The trail here was very steep and rocky but the views made it all worthwhile. Shortly after leaving Namche we got our first peak at Everest—wow! We made a stop at one village to visit the Sherpa Museum—dedicated to all the brave souls who have helped guide climbers to their destination. This was housed in two buildings—the first held a collection of old Sherpa household implements and articles of clothing; the second a wonderful collection of photos of Nepali life as well as photos of various Everest expeditions. Sir Edmund Hillary dedicated this museum in 1993.

On the fourth day we arrived at the Tengboche Monastery—the goal of many trekkers, such as ourselves, who are not continuing to Everest base camp. This is the largest and most active monastery in the region. I was led to a bed in a very sunny dormitory which had a window looking out on the snowy peaks. Despite the sun, it was *very* cold. When I woke up the next morning the temperature registered just above freezing (in the room!). After a hot breakfast, however, I felt a bit warmer and decided to see if there really *was* a "hot shower" as promised. I asked a girl who was drying her hair, and she said "yes." So off I trotted to the shower room, carrying a large basin to catch water for my laundry afterwards. When I turned on the faucet—voila—hot water! I happily cleansed my body of trail debris, but just as I was about to apply shampoo to my wet head the water stopped. Thank goodness I was not all soaped up. I dried off as quickly as I could in the freezing cold room and put on clean clothes (a real treat). I Then took my basin of warm water outside and washed my dirty clothes which I took back to my sunny room to dry—as best as possible. They would have frozen if I had left them outside. Again, I obviously did not take this trip for the amenities it offered! The monastery itself was gorgeous inside— beautifully decorated with painted walls and ceilings, and many *thanka* paintings (which represented symbolic religious expressions). Lording over all was a large seated Buddha. While we were there, the head lama of the entire region and his entourage happened to come by. Pemba went over and touched his robe—a lovely moment for him and a significant memory for me as my Nepalese adventure was coming to an end. The only thing left was the trek back to Lukla and the various flights back to the U.S.A.

Vietnam and Cambodia

—————

IT'S GOOD TO HAVE FRIENDS WHO ALSO LOVE INTERNATIONAL travel. December 6, 2006 found me aboard a United Airlines flight to Saigon (or Ho Chi Min City, if you will). I had never been that keen about visiting Southeast Asia, but the opportunity came up so I grabbed it. My physician friend, "Dr. Jan," had been doing volunteer work for the past six months at a hospital in Hanoi and invited me to join her in her last two weeks abroad. Vietnam here I come!

Due to the international date line, I didn't arrive in Saigon until December 7. The arrivals area was a madhouse, so I was extremely glad to spot Jan as I neared the exit. She had a taxi waiting which whisked us into town in about half-an-hour. I was also very grateful to have the benefit of her knowledge of the country as I didn't even know how to say "hello" in Vietnamese. I will interject at this time that while hiking with Jan the year before in Oregon, she brought along her Vietnamese language book and would study while waiting up for me.

Jan had had an affinity for Vietnam for some time and was even considering adopting a native child (red tape did not allow for this to happen). She did, however take on preliminary medical care of a 12-year-old she met in an orphanage near Hanoi. She had noticed the girl's swollen neck glands and suspected lymphoma. As major medical facilities were not available in the girl's village, Jan arranged for her to take the 12-hour bus ride to Saigon and get a biopsy at a major hospital there. Consequently, my first morning in town was spent at this hospital while the girl underwent the procedure—not your usual tourist attraction, but interesting in its own way. Fortunately, the girl did not have cancer, just the probability of TB, which was a whole lot better as that is quite treatable. Jan agreed to oversee her treatment from the States.

After this medical excursion, we had a day-and-a-half in town before heading south to the Mekong Delta. The traffic was crazy. There are only a handful of traffic control devices, and the streets are awhirl with activity. If you waited for traffic to clear before crossing a street you would never get across. The majority of vehicles were motorscooters, although there was also a fair amount of cars. You simply step out into the mix and attempt to make eye contact with the drivers. They are very adept at steering around you. We also used these motorscooters as our local transportation—not as drivers, but as passengers—on occasion. All you have to do is raise your hand and one or more will come to your service. You simply hop up on the seat behind the driver and hold on for dear life. On my first ride, I had my driver in a death grip and had to close my eyes at times as he adroitly avoided those pesky pedestrians!

There is a good deal of French influence in Saigon. Notre Dame Cathedral was particularly interesting—especially its neon-lighted chapels. And the main post office was beautiful with its classic lines and vaulted ceiling. A huge Christmas tree adorned the lobby. Christmas is very big in Viet Nam—not for religious reasons, but for the colors, lights, and gifts. We sat at a sidewalk café and listened to carols being sung with an Asian accent. During this trip downtown we also visited the Palace of Reunification (the commie name given to the Presidential Palace after the fall of South Vietnam in 1975) and the War Remnants Museum (where the U.S. is depicted as the "bad guys"). These displays were sobering. On a positive note, there was an exhibit of children's drawings depicting world peace.

Our day trip to the Mekong Delta took us 70 kilometers south of Saigon where we hopped on a small boat and explored various watery byways, stopping at several islands for short walks through tropical foliage. We later enjoyed lunch and made a "snake stop" where I was draped with a real, live boa (actually, I think they said it was a python). Instead of returning to Saigon by bus, we opted to take the Saigon River back to town. As we motored slowly along we saw a lot of dredging activity—huge scows piled high with gravel being transported upriver. The workers live on small boats with their clothes hanging on the outside flapping in the breeze (obviously, no closets!). The closer to the city we got, the more hovels there were lining the riverbanks. They were some of the poorest dwellings I've ever encountered in my world travels.

Before heading north out of Saigon for the Central Highlands, we hooked up with the local Hash House Harriers. Since it's impossible to run in the city, they hire a bus which takes the group about an hour out of town and drops everyone off at a village where the run (and fun) begins. There was great camaraderie as we slogged along muddy water buffalo tracks and crossed a stream via a "monkey bridge" (this consisted of slippery tree limbs lashed together with an attempt at a handrail). With muddy running shoes, it was quite the challenge to get across. One of the local Hashers was off to the side with a camera to "catch" anyone who fell off, but no one did! After the run we partook in the obligatory beer drinking and bawdy songs with great gusto and then back to town.

Next on the agenda was a visit to the town of Dalat in the Central Highlands. Dalat lies at an elevation of about 2,500 feet where the weather is considerably cooler than the 90-some degrees in Saigon. After an 8-hour bus trip (ugh!) we arrived at this very popular Vietnamese tourist town. Many locals like to get married here because of its (kind of) Swiss chalet ambience, although I don't think a Swiss person would recognize it as such. In any case, we found ourselves a swell hotel near the town's lovely lake and headed down the block to a restaurant mentioned in Lonely Planet (our "bible"). Here we spotted a brochure featuring "jungle treks," so the next morning we hit the trail for an 8-mile turn through the local flora (didn't see much fauna). It was just Jan and I and two guides. Lots of ups and downs, with lunch about half-way provided by the guides (bread, cheese, pork pate, and fruit—yum!). We wound up descending through a coffee plantation. At the end, a car was waiting to take us back to town. The next morning Jan and I jogged the four miles around the city's lake. I didn't get any comments (as in 1982) but I'm sure the locals were quite surprised to see an "old lady" hoofing it around their lake sporting an Oregon Ducks T-shirt (whatever *that* meant!).

Probably the highlight of our trip was a visit to the temples of Cambodia around Angkor Wat. I had seen many photos of this world-famous site but never really expected to see the real thing. It was a fabulous experience. We took the 50-minute flight from Saigon to Siem Reap (gateway town for the temples), arriving in the early evening. Our taxi driver, Mr. T, drove us into town where we found a great hotel for $20 (air-conditioning, private bath, and nice view). He then asked if we needed further transportation while in town, which, of course, we did. He mentioned his friend Mr.

Soth who could take us around in his motorbike "rickshaw." This conveyance was exactly what it sounds like—a traditional-looking rickshaw pulled by a motorbike instead of a human. This arrangement turned out perfectly. Mr. Soth arrived at our hotel promptly at 9:00 the next morning and was at our disposal for the next three days (at $12 a day). Jan and I sat back like royalty in our cushioned "carriage" while he drove us hither and yon. The temples were about half-an-hour from town. He would stop at the various sights and wait while we looked around. Some of the temples were quite well-maintained while nature is slowly reclaiming others. Some go back at least 1,000 years. The intricacy of the carving is amazing. The next morning Jan and I were once again back at the temple grounds—this time to run the Angkor Wat 10K. We didn't plan our trip around this event. It just happened to be taking place while we were there—what a coup! Mr. Soth picked us up at 5:15 a.m. The race started early, at 6:30, because of the hot and muggy weather. We arrived at the start just before dawn and were rewarded with the sight of the new day emerging from the darkness above the towers of Angkor Wat—a never-to-be-forgotten scene! The race was put on for the benefit of land-mine amputees (to provide prostheses for them). A number of these folks ran the race, and several of them beat me! I was in no particular hurry as there were no age-group awards. Awards were given to the top five overall only. After the race Jan and I once again met up with Mr. Soth. We needed some-place to change out of our wet shirts, and in looking around didn't see any private spots. Mr. Soth soon understood our dilemma and lowered the side flaps on his rickshaw for our privacy—a most unique dressing room!

On our last day in the area we took a boat ride on a river where people live on floating platforms—extremely primitive. The school was also afloat, as well as a basketball court! Fishing seemed to be the main industry (in addition to tourism). Dozens of boats were lined up waiting to take tourists down the river to the entrance of Lake Tonle Sap. There, they turn around and go back up river. Jan wanted to make a stop at an environmental center. She was feeling sad about the poverty and was glad to see that efforts are being made to improve the lot of the locals (sanitation, etc.). The highlight of the day, however, was a visit to Mr. Soth's home. He asked if we would like to do this, and we responded with an enthusiastic "yes!" It was a real insight into a local's life (and he lives well above the standards of the river folk). His thatched-roof home was on stilts. You climbed a kind of ladder to the entrance. Inside was one main room, with a curtained-off area containing a mattress on the floor. There was no furniture in the main room—just mats on the floor and hammocks strung along one wall. Mr. Soth lives here with his wife, three children, and his mother-in-law (who got the mattress). Through an opening, we could see the kitchen area with containers of food on the floor. Cooking was done over a wood fire. Water was carried up the ladder from below. Every morning Mr. Soth fills basins of water and pours them into a ceramic cistern for daily use. We Americans should never complain about minor inconveniences! Anyway, when we arrived, Mr. Soth's oldest son, about 10, scurried up a coconut tree and got us our refreshment; Mr. Soth then hacked the coconuts open and took them upstairs for us to enjoy. Hospitality comes in many forms around the world.

The final chapter of the trip was almost a disaster for me. We arrived back from Cambodia to Viet Nam in the early evening. Jan and I were in adjacent lines going through immigration. She passed through first and I expected to follow momentarily. But no, that was not to be. The official at the counter stopped me. I had no idea what was going on. After some moments of "no English spoken" he circled a notation on my passport that said "one entry" (into Viet Nam). I was under the impression that my visa was good for 30 days, which it was) but I could only come into the country once (and I had already done that when I first arrived). They were not about to let me through. Jan was just on the other side of the barrier so I could tell her what was going on. The official then indicated for me to go over to another counter and talk to someone else. This time there was a fair amount of English understood. I explained that I was leaving the country in two days, and he asked to see my ticket. In my current state of unrest I pawed through my belongings several times and could not find the ticket. I then asked Jan to go to baggage claim and see if it was in my bag. She returned in about 20 minutes and said it was not. Not until late that night did it finally dawn on me that I had never gotten a paper ticket for my return ticket (e-ticket only). What I did have, however, was a computer print-out of my itinerary which I showed to the guy. At first he said I was going to have to leave the country immediately. This would have been horrible, as I would have had to forfeit my original air ticket and buy a new one at great expense. He then made a phone call and returned to tell me I could stay the next two days, but it would have to be at a "transit hotel" where I would have to remain until leaving (relinquishing my passport until my departure date). Unfortunately, the transit hotel was a 4-star palace that cost $100 a night (Jan and I had already booked at a 2-star for $25 a night), but I had absolutely no choice. Jan was a sweetheart and stayed with me at the transit hotel the first night (I would have felt quite bereft to have been dumped there by myself—even it *was* a 4-star!) Thus we made lemonade out of lemons. The next morning we enjoyed a lavish breakfast in the tasteful dining room (included in room cost). Jan then left to take care of some last minute items (like buying a few more Christmas presents). I proceeded to spend the day at the hotel enjoying the many amenities of my deluxe digs. I was not fitted with any kind of restraining device and seemed free to wander at will. I first went to the 8th floor fitness center and hopped on a treadmill—enjoying a great view of the city as I jogged. Then a visit to the pool where the cool water felt delightful. After my dip I stretched out on a chaise longue and read for a couple of hours. My final activity was a full body massage—for $5.00! I couldn't believe the price when I saw it listed in a brochure in my room, but it was true. I was led by a guy to a small, dimly-lit massage room with soft Oriental music playing through speakers. He then handed me a towel and closed the door. I wasn't sure what to do but figured I should probably take off my clothes, which I did, and then climbed up on the table with the towel over me. In a few minutes there was a discrete knock and a young woman entered (I was very happy that it was not the young guy). English did not seem to be part of the mix, but she indicated for me to turn over (on my stomach). She then jumped up on the table and straddled my thighs. Oh my—I wasn't sure what to expect next!

After the initial shock I thought, "Oh well, when in Saigon…" She first started working on my back, then slid down a bit, whipped the towel off my butt and began working on that part of my anatomy. After that she got off the table and manipulated my arms, fingers, legs, toes, face (including ears) and scalp. I certainly got my five dollars worth! Feeling totally relaxed, I returned to my room and enjoyed two Heinekens from the mini-bar while watching the news on CNN (they don't soak you like the mini-bars in the States—the beers cost only $1.36 each).

After an early dinner, I turned in around 8:30. My wake-up call was for 3:00 a.m. with departure for the airport at 3:45. In the morning I made coffee in the room and polished off a yogurt I had taken from yesterday's bountiful breakfast. When I went downstairs a car was waiting to whisk me to the airport by 4:00 (flight at 6:05). During the drive all I could do was pray that my passport would be returned. My first stop was the United Airlines counter where the agent asked for my passport. Explaining my situation, he told me to go upstairs to immigration. I didn't pass another soul in the pre-dawn environment. It was quite eerie. At first I didn't see anyone in the immigration area, but eventually spotted one lone official leaning sleepily against a counter. Walking over to him, I said in as firm a voice as I could manage, "I'm here to pick up my passport." To my amazement (and immense relief), he simply asked my name, went over to a cupboard, unlocked a door and returned with my passport! I felt like giving him a bear hug and a huge smooch, but thought that might frighten him away. Instead, I simply smiled sweetly and said "thank you." Some 26 hours later I arrived back in Eugene to a lovely, rainy, wintery day—ah, home sweet home!

Bhutan (Land of Gross National Happiness) or Prayer Flags and Power Poles

———

HOW COULD I NOT VISIT A LAND WHOSE MOTTO IS "GROSS national happiness?" In December of 2011, I once again joined a Road Scholar group and spent two wonderful weeks exploring this unique country. As a world-traveler, I have visited many unusual and out-of-the-way places, but Bhutan was one-of-a-kind. It's on the ground floor of emergence into the modern world. Is this a good thing? Let's hope so. It will be a real challenge for the country to "emerge" while still maintaining its cultural heritage. I sub-titled this piece "Prayer Flags and Power Poles" because those are the two things that the visitor sees in abundance while taking in the sights. The prayer flags have been there forever. The power poles only now becoming more and more a part of the landscape as modernization takes place. Bhutan charts its progress according to the country's Gross National Happiness index. It's not happiness in the Western sense of wealth and possessions, rather in the Buddhist way of contentment. Bhutan is roughly the size of Switzerland, surrounded by China and India, with a population of around 700,000. The towering peaks of the Himalayas mark its northern boundary while the south experiences considerable heat and humidity during the monsoon season. It's definitely a country of geographical and climatic contrasts. An ideal time to visit is October, but the trip I wanted to sign up for at that time was full, so I had to be content with an early December departure. I was a bit concerned about being cold, but needn't have been. By the time we got going each morning it was well above freezing and sometimes even warmed up into the mid-60s with, usually, an abundance of bright sunshine.

Getting there from my home in Eugene was *not* "half the fun." It began with an afternoon flight to LAX, arriving at 6:40 p.m. Then a 3-1/2 hour wait for the first leg of the far east journey. Finally, at 10:20 p.m., our Cathay Pacific plane roared to life and headed for Hong Kong (arriving 15 hours later—aargh!). This was followed by a 3-hour layover in Hong Kong while awaiting the final 3-hour leg to Bangkok where we would spend the night. I figured that from the time I had gotten up in Eugene until landing in Bangkok some 38 hours had elapsed! Fortunately, the Road Scholar folks were there to meet us zombies and take us to a nearby hotel where I immediately zonked out. When my roommate woke me later she said it was 6 o'clock. I didn't know if she meant a.m. or p.m. Totally disoriented, I splashed some water on my face and managed to stagger downstairs for what turned out to be a delicious Thai dinner (not breakfast). I wasn't about to miss a meal, whatever it was!

The next morning we were back at the airport for the final hop to Bhutan on Drukair (Druk meaning dragon). Our entry into Paro—site of Bhutan's only airport—was an experience in itself as the pilot masterfully guided the plane between two mountainsides without scraping anything. Drukair has only two planes in its fleet—offering service to Bangkok and New Delhi. Once through Customs and Immigration our group was met by Finn (his English name), Sonam, and Dorji—our incredible guides for the next two weeks. Dorji, the driver, should be bestowed with the AAA medal for "Best Driver of the Year." Motoring along Bhutan's one and only trans-country road is not for the faint-hearted or ill-prepared (more on this later),

Our group of twelve then hopped onto our own little bus and were driven to Thimpu (the capital city), some 45 minutes north-east. A short drive through town and then up a dusty, rutted road led us to our lovely hotel—much fancier than I had expected. I was later told that the reason for such first class hotels in Bhutan is that they are built for tourists. The local folks, if and when they travel, stay in "one-stars" or less. Anyway, after my roommate and

I rested up a bit we walked the short distance back to town to take a look at "rush-hour" traffic. There are no traffic lights in Bhutan. We watched a highly-efficient, smartly-uniformed "traffic cop" as he used an amazing variety of hand signals to keep traffic flowing. He stood at the one major intersection in town where several roads converged. It was quite the ballet! Then back to the hotel for our first Bhutanese meal in the hotel dining room. This was typical of meals to follow on our journey—always a large pan of rice, a meat or chicken option (or both) and lots of veggies. It was served buffet-style, each person taking just what they wanted. For the adventurous souls there was always a "hot" item—the Bhutanese love chilies. I passed.

The next day, somewhat recovered from jet lag, we visited a nearly chorten (a Bhutanese spiritual monument) situated high on a hill. After taking in the prayer wheels, prayer flags and other religious accouterments we next visited the world's largest "outside" Buddha (about 15 stories high). Big Buddha looked very benevolent, peacefully gazing out over his realm. At the foot of the monument, Indian laborers were busily working to construct a fitting base for this very important statue (much of Bhutan's physical labor comes from next door India). In the afternoon we visited an incredibly-primitive paper-making facility. Everything here is done by hand—from treating the bark to artwork (if any) on the finished product. Outside the building, a wood-fueled furnace burns brightly to heat large vats of water used for processing the bark. Inside, workers are busy at various stations of production. Our last day in Thimpu found us at a wonderful textile museum. The Bhutanese are known for their fine weaving and beautiful, colorful products. And later that afternoon we visited an impressive dzong (prior fortress) which now houses the administrative headquarters of the government of Bhutan. The king lives nearby in a very modest house. Bhutan is ruled by a constitutional monarchy—everyone seems to get along and work well with one another. Take notice world!

The following day we headed east for the 6-hour drive to the Phob-jikha Valley on "Highway 1" (the *only* highway in the country) where the speed limit is 15 MPH! We had been forewarned about this road, but as long as one observes the speed limit everything's just fine. The road is made up of, principally, a long, long series of almost continual switchbacks (sometimes requiring backing up on a particularly tight curve). As I stated earlier, our driver was a pro. Dorji took it all in stride, managing not to run into roadside cows (of which there were many) or vehicles coming in the opposite direction (of which there were few). The scenery was wonderful. We were either surrounded by forests, with views of occasional cascading waterfalls, or were looking down on endless valleys. Since there are no "rest areas" in Bhutan we had "tea and pee" breaks. The "tea" part usually once or twice a day. The "pee" part more often. I was very glad I had my hiking stick with me as it was often necessary to navigate some very uneven terrain in order to find a bit of privacy (men on one side of the bus, women on the other).

We were now in the territory of Bhutan's famed black-necked cranes—regarded as heavenly by Buddhists. These beautiful birds fly south from Tibet and spend the winter in this more temperate Bhutanese valley. We happened to be there at just the right time! We got a good, if somewhat distant, view of them as we hiked in the area. Our rooms at the hotel that night were heated by wood stoves (with hot water bottles being tucked into our beds while we were at dinner). Electricity in this area has been a long time coming (although there is now lighting—most of the time). A major reason for this was concern that electric wires might disturb the crane's annual migration—wow! I must relate an amusing incident that occurred at this hotel. When I got up in the "wee" hours I went into the bathroom and turned on the light. While I was comfortably seated, the electricity went out and it suddenly became pitch dark. Not having committed the floor plan to memory, I found myself trying to get into my roommate's bed on the return trip. Excusing myself, after getting a surprised grunt from her, I got down on my butt on the floor and scuttled across the room until I found my own bed!

After two days in this area, we continued east, crossing over Pele La (a pass at 11,000 ft.—the highest point on our trip). On the way down from the pass we visited a school (grades 4-6) and observed the children. We first saw them at play on a dry, dusty field and then in a flag-raising ceremony (which takes place every morning). The students, smartly dressed in their colorful native garb, line up and sing the national anthem once the flag is raised. It was a joy to see their tasteful clothing instead of the sloppy jeans and T-shirts so often worn by American students. The boys wear a *gho* (a piece of woven material that drapes around the body from the shoulders to the knees and down the arms with wide white cuffs. Knee-high socks and western shoes complete the outfit. The girls wear a *kira* (an ankle-length slim skirt topped with a jacket—often of different patterns and colors. As I mentioned earlier, the Bhutanese love color and design.

Continuing down the hill we were taken to a private home for lunch. We entered into the living room/kitchen (bedroom at night) and were directed to sit on cushions on the floor with our backs to the wall. The only furniture seemed to be a couple of shelving units used for kitchen utensils. However…there was a TV near the stove—wonder what kind of programming they get! Unfortunately, the residents were outside working, but a young boy (presumably their son) was home as well as a friendly cat who seemed very interested in our chicken lunch. The building was 2-story—with the living quarters downstairs and a grain storage area and "shrine room" (as colorfully decorated as some of the temples we've visited) upstairs. The stairway, almost a ladder, required our full attention.

Retracing our steps to Thimpu on Highway 1, we paid a visit to the Watchtower Museum which overlooks the Trongsa Dzong below. The museum is constructed of multiple levels as one climbs to a lookout at the top (each level exhibiting various artifacts from the past). The view of the valley below from the lookout was fantastic. After absorbing this grand scene we trotted back downstairs and then continued our descent down a steep path to the Tronsga Dzong itself. When we arrived we were fortunate to observe a group of villagers rehearsing in the courtyard for an upcoming national festival. The dances involved a lot of hopping and balancing on one leg—definitely not for me! We also saw several monkeys scampering along the ex-fortress walls which added to the atmosphere. This dzong is the ancestral home of the royal family (no longer used as such). On the walk back to the bus we were very lucky to witness a bit of archery—Bhutan's national sport. The target is 150 meters away!

Another interesting day was spent at the Temple of the Divine Madman. A short hike through rice paddies led us to this intriguing-sounding edifice. This guy is one of Bhutan's favorite saints. He was a rogue Buddhist preacher who used outrageous behavior to get people to discard their religious preconceptions and learn the true teachings of Buddha. His persuasion included lots of sexual references and practices and is the basis for the phallus being prominently displayed on many structures in Bhutan today (at the edges of roofs or as artistic wall paintings). Replicas are also on sale as souvenirs (of various sizes) in gift shops.

Before leaving the country we were treated to a very unexpected celestial event—a total lunar eclipse. One evening, not long after we had retired, we were awakened by loud knocking on our doors and told to look outside. There, we saw the townspeople gathered in the street dancing and yelling. Legend has it that demons took away the moon and that all the shouting will bring it back. I guess it worked because the moon eventually reappeared.

Our final destination before leaving the country was a visit to Tiger's Nest. This is Bhutan's iconic monastery perched on a rocky cliffside (many a travel office sports its photo). The approximate 2-3 hours climb begins at 8,000 feet and ends at 10,000 feet. A tea house half way affords a bit of rest and sustenance (tea and crackers). Near the end, the path turns to stone steps—750 of them! They first lead down and then up to the entrance to the monastery. It was amazing to me to actually be standing in this place I had only seen in phonographs. Hundreds and hundreds of prayer flags flapping in the breeze added to the ambience. There was tight security before entering—no cameras or cell phones—and we were even frisked! We then wandered in and out of a number of rooms depicting various aspects of Buddhism (impossible to keep it all straight). On the way back down we stopped at a certain point and were served a hot lunch which had been brought up by pack horses. I've never had that kind of meal service on a hike—a truly memorable day! In conclusion, I just want to say to the Bhutanese—keep those prayer flags and power poles in balance!

CHAPTER 19

THE MIDDLE EAST

Perambulating through Persia

PEOPLE ALWAYS ASK ME WHEN I RETURN FROM ONE OF MY trips, "Where are you going next, Jane?" I never have an answer. I have no bucket list, though at (almost) 83 perhaps I should put one together so as not to miss any place really important to me. In any case, I simply say, "I'll read something, see something on TV, or just talk to someone." Well, in the Spring of 2018 I happened to be chatting with a well-traveled friend who casually mentioned that he had visited Iran the year before and asked if I had ever considered going there. I answered, "no." With all the unrest in that part of the world I hadn't really given it a thought, but Michael is a truly intrepid traveler, having led bike trips in Europe when he was younger, and I would take very seriously any travel suggestion he might make. Now that he had presented me with this idea, it quickly caught fire, began to smolder and soon was burning bright. To go to a place so few Americans visit and have a look at a different culture really appealed to me. The following day I signed up for a trip taking place that Fall. It didn't hurt that there was an "early bird" discount as I am always looking for the best bang for my buck (or in this case *rial*). My next call was to my erstwhile travel buddy Fran in Vermont who is almost always up for something different. And this would certainly be *different*. Never mind that the State Department did not recommend travel to Iran at this time. I always figure that if a tour group is planning a trip, they most likely plan to come back home from wherever it is they go. And Fran is equally optimistic.

We were a small group of 11 based in Eugene, Oregon. Fran and a professor from Princeton were the two east coast participants. It was an archaeology-based trip as so much of Iran is blessed with amazing remains of ancient civilizations—Persepolis being the crown jewel. I don't have a major interest in antiquity, but I must say it was pretty impressive to gaze at what was around thousands of years ago and is still visible today—in spite of weather, wars, and earthquakes. Our little group took off on October 16, from opposite coasts, headed for Tehran (any earlier in the year can be uncomfortably hot). It was a grueling 24-hour+ journey consisting of three separate flights (Eugene-San Francisco-Frankfurt-Tehran) for the west-coasters. Before we landed at Imam Khomeini International Airport an announcement came on reminding women to be sure and cover their heads before deplaning. We had been well-advised about this Muslim requirement and dutifully popped out our head scarves (the more encompassing *hijab* was, fortunately, not required). Bare arms and legs are also a no-no, so long sleeves and long pants—with a loose blouse or smock covering the butt—is the preferred dress. This was no big deal, and we were happy to comply with this cultural/religious requirement.

Our 17-day sojourn began in Tehran. I was very surprised at the traffic—almost as bad as L.A. (with lane-lines being more or less a suggestion). From there we traveled by our own private bus through what seemed like the entire country. The 12-hour days tended to be grueling, and I would have preferred a few fewer sights and a little down time each day to kick back and relax. The archeologists among us, however, seemed to eat up everything they threw at us. Fortunately, we stayed at least two nights in each hotel so we didn't have to pack and unpack each day. And the hotels were excellent—no complaints there. They even provided WI-FI—which surprised me—but no Facebook allowed in Iran! At least we could keep up with our email. Breakfast was always at the hotel as was dinner most nights. My favorite breakfast turned out to be creamy yogurt with a dollop of "carrot marmalade" mixed in—delicious. This I topped off with flat bread and cheese. One of our dinner stops was an Italian restaurant. I didn't feel like Italian food so ordered a cheeseburger, which was an unlikely offering on the menu. I guess they wanted to cater to various foreign "cuisines." It was delicious. Some of my table mates eyed it covetously! This was served with fries—which happily surprised me. Almost jokingly, I asked if they had any ketchup. In moments I was brought several packets! Nothing like a cheeseburger at an Italian restaurant in Iran! When we had dinner at the hotels there was always a salad bar—with an amazing number of choices—to which we helped ourselves. The main courses were then brought to the table which we shared family-style. These always included massive platters of rice adorned with saffron and plates of chicken, meat, or vegetable concoctions. One night I was told we had camel—oh, dear! Many times the seasonings were unfamiliar, but always quite good. My overall impression of Iranian cuisine, however, was that it was rather bland. I almost always added salt and pepper.

Our two days in Tehran at the start of the trip consisted mainly of visiting mosques and museums. One of my favorites being the Stones and Bones Museum which showcased exactly what it was named for—artifacts from local digs—some dating back 12,000 years. My favorite display was an ancient bull which had its belly supported by a contraption to help keep him upright! Your belly would sag, too, if you were a few thousand years old! Our sightseeing was strictly overseen. We could go nowhere without our official guide. Fortunately, Medhi was a very well-informed and personable guy. Before leaving the city for our trek around the country we paid a visit to the Iranian Crown Jewels tucked away deep inside the Central Bank of Iran. The security here was as tight as at airports. You could carry NOTHING inside! The splendor was dazzling. It's amazing to view the ostentatiousness of the super-rich. One exhibit was a large golden globe with the oceans made of emeralds!

From Tehran we headed to Susa where we visited a Unesco-listed archaeological site dating back 6,000 years. It was once similar in scale to Persepolis but is now greatly reduced in scope. Here we paid a visit to Daniel's Tomb (remember the lions' den?). The current structure dates from 1871 though the tradition surrounding Daniel's relics dates back over 1,000 years. This tomb would make Liberace proud. It was extremely elaborate and shiny. It was also extremely holy. Women were required to drape themselves in an additional garment while viewing it.

From Susa we had a l-o-n-g drive to Shiraz. If I had one word to describe Iranian landscape it would be "brown." We drove miles and miles through flat, dusty terrain. Peoples' homes have no landscaping. They appeared to be just bare structures on dusty roads. In fact it was often difficult to distinguish residences from businesses. Businesses were often housed in structures that looked like single-car garages placed side by side where closing up meant lowering the "front door." Upon reaching Shiraz we did encounter some greenery which most cities make an effort to cultivate as best they can. For 2,000 years Shiraz has been known as the epicenter of Persian civilization. It was arguably the most important city in the medieval Islamic world and today is best known for being a next-door neighbor to Persepolis—one of the great wonders of the ancient world and now a major tourist site. Persepolis was conceived by Darius the Great who in 520 BC inherited the responsibility for ruling the world's first known empire founded by his predecessor, Cyrus the Great. The result is an eclectic set of structures, including monumental staircases, exquisite reliefs and imposing gateways. Darius' impressive tomb is located some 12 km from Persepolis high up on a rocky hillside at Naqsh-e Rostam (alongside three other high mucky-mucks of the day). The visit to this area would have been perfect if only the vineyards of Shiraz were still being cultivated!

Another long, hot drive (which included a flat tire) took us to the City of Kerman. Fortunately, our bus was nicely air-conditioned (and the driver new how to fix a flat!) Here we visited its famed, 1,200-foot-long covered bazaar -site of an ancient trading post. It was fascinating to wander through and look at all the merchandise for sale, which included some modern western clothes in its displays. My only purchase was a small towel to replace the washcloth I left at the first hotel in Tehran. I'm sure I'm the only person in Eugene to have a Persian face cloth hanging over my tub!

Next on the agenda was a visit to Yazd—a desert city with atmospheric alleys and historic lanes through which we strolled. An interesting aspect of this area is that about 10% of the populace follows the ancient religion of Zoroastrianism. An elegant *ateshkadeh* (fire temple) nearby shelters an eternal flame, symbolic of this religion, which we visited. Afterwards we drove to the "towers of silence"— earth mounds where the Zoroastrians placed their dead to be consumed by vultures. They believed that dead bodies contaminated the earth. This practice is not being observed today—although it makes a lot of sense to me! Before leaving Yazd, we were introduced to a totally different activity. Our guide said he was taking us to a "gym." Did he feel we needed some exercise to counteract the long bus rides? No, he wanted to show us a choreographed exercise routine practiced by Iranian males. We entered a building that looked nothing like a gym. It was a single room with folding chairs lined up against the wall. These looked onto a lowered "pit" where the guys were warming up for their routine. There were about about 20 of them—ranging in age from about 7 to 70. After this brief warm-up they began the routine—squats, push-ups, jumps, twirls—performed to the beat of a drum and chant of a vocalist. The intensity was, of course, age-appropriate. It was quite amazing to watch. What caught my eye immediately, beside their movements, was their clothing. They were all attired in paisley-decorated knee-length pants—so different from boring American "sweats!" After the performance I asked our guide if I could get a pair, and so I did. Normally, women do not wear these as they have no corresponding exercise program available and have no need for them. Of course, I didn't let this bother me. I guessed at a size which turned out to be almost perfect. I love my beautiful Iranian workout pants!

After another long, dusty drive, a stop in Esfahan took us on foot across two major bridges that crossed over a dry riverbed—the water was needed elsewhere and had been diverted. About half-way across one of them we heard singing and stopped to have a listen. A group of people had gathered under one of the arches to listen to some local musicians—very atmospheric! The second bridge contained 31 arches over which we walked. As we made our way across we were stopped several times by locals asking if they could take photos with us. So much for "Death to America!" We stood there smiling, with our arms around each other. If only the world could get along like this. If it was up to "the people" it would!

One of our last stops before returning to Tehran was Abyan-ech Village—an ancient village still inhabited—where many the elderly residents speak Middle Persian and wear traditional garb. It's a fascinating place of twisting lanes and crumbling red adobe houses. We spent a couple of hours here while munching on dried apples—a local treat—and then headed to Kashan. Here we sampled another bazaar and visited an enormous private home (no longer inhabited) containing four courtyards and some stunning interior mirrors and glasswork—again, Liberace would have been proud! Our last dinner on the road, that evening, took place at the food court of a very modern mall (could have been in the US!).

Back in Tehran, we had one more day of sightseeing scheduled. I opted out, much preferring to hang out in the comfort of my room and rest before the exhausting trip back home, starting late that evening. Our guide told me to please not leave the hotel. He needn't have been concerned. I had no desire to go anywhere. I happily read and rested. In the afternoon I headed down to the lobby to sit for a while. On the way there I missed a step walking down a slippery marble hallway. Unable to cushion my fall, I pitched forward and landed hard on my chest. Two young hotel employees rushed over to help the "old lady"- guiding me to a seat and bringing me some water. I think they were just as relieved as I was that no permanent damage seemed to have been done. How this would effect my long flight later that evening remained to be seen (it didn't, to any great extent). My back and chest felt very sore, but I could manage.

If I thought the 24+ hours travel time from Eugene to Tehran was bad, I had no idea what I was in for on the return journey. We left the hotel around 10 p.m. for the airport—an hour's drive away. With a 2:50 a.m. scheduled departure time scheduled, this would get us there in plenty of time—having been told to arrive three hours ahead of time. Ironically, time is something we wound up having more than enough of. Upon arrival, we were told that our flight out of Tehran was 4-1/2 hours delayed (no reason given). This, of course, screwed up everyone's connections which meant we all had to get in a long line to get re-booked. As I was standing there looking forlorn, an agent came up to me and said to sit down and that he would handle the transaction for me. Hey, I didn't ask for it, but if someone wants to hand me the "age card" I'll happily take it (and I'm sure that's what happened). After about 20 minutes he returned with my new booking. And not only was I re-booked, but I had been upgraded to "business class" for the 5-hour flight between Tehran and Frankfurt (I actually got a bit of sleep). The nearly 12-hour flight between Frankfurt and Eugene, however, had not been upgraded. At that point I was willing to pay the $800 difference, but there was no space available. Despite all this shuffling around, I arrived in Eugene only 2-1/2 hours later than originally scheduled, but whether it was A.M. or P.M. I couldn't tell you for sure. It had been over 30 hours since I had gotten out of bed in Tehran! I was never happier to see anyone than I was to spot my wonderful cat-sitter, Beverly, who was waiting for me in the arrivals area.

CHAPTER 20

THE ARCTIC AND
THE ANTARCTIC

Above the Arctic Circle

IN 2011, IN SEARCH OF A NEW ADVENTURE, I WAS BROWSING through an Elderhostel (now Road Scholar) brochure and came upon a trip to the Arctic. I had been to Alaska, but not above the Arctic Circle, so this definitely intrigued me. The group met at the University of Fairbanks where we were lodged for several days in their dorms while exploring the local environs. Then the dozen-or-so of us motored up the Dalton Highway to the Prudhoe Bay oilfields. This road was known as the "haul road" during the construction of the pipeline (between 1975 and 1977) to service the construction workers. The 789-mile road is not paved because of the inherent problems with permafrost, but it is very well-graded so the ride was quite smooth. The scenery was out of this world as we headed north through the magnificent wilderness. Besides the rugged scenery it was amazing to get up-close views of the enormous, snaking pipeline (4 feet in diameter). What a project that must have been for the workers. In the winter they had to work inside temporary enclosures to keep from freezing. As we drove through in July, however, it was a very different story. We were having about 23 hours of sunshine. In fact, the places where we stayed all had thick drapes to keep out the sun at night so we could sleep! Along the way to Prudhoe Bay we stopped to visit the homestead of a "sustainer." These are folks who live totally off the grid and sustain themselves from the land. Unfortunately, this man's wife had died some years before and he had simply buried her next to the house (marked by a small cross). He was now bringing up two kids on his own. He did have one modern appliance, however—an electronic mosquito zapper! The little buggers are fierce in this neck of the woods.

When we arrived at Prudhoe Bay we were taken to our lodgings—the leftover trailers of the construction workers, now fitted out for tourists. They were totally comfortable. Meals were taken in the "dining trailer" and were excellent. We were told that some of the "construction cooks" stayed on to work for the tourists. And the reason that the food was so good was that the pipeline workers had demanded it. It was their only real pleasure during their arduous work under very hostile conditions.

A highlight of this part of the trip was a look at (and a dip in) the Arctic Ocean. I had brought along a bathing suit for full immersion, but when I dipped my toes in the water and looked out at chunks of ice floating nearby I changed my mind. I went in up to my knees only. Several of our group did make the full plunge and got certificates to prove it! On the return trip to Fairbanks we flew in two small planes. Our route over the Brooks Range was spectacular. In these small planes you felt as though you could almost reach out and touch the mountains. When the weather is overcast this is not the case, but we were blessed with a beautiful, clear day. After the oilfields and our return to Fairbanks we had one last item on the agenda—a bit of trail maintenance on the Iditarod Trail near Anchorage (this is the famous trail that takes mushers on a 1,000-mile trek from Anchorage to Nome every spring). Our 360-mile rail journey from Fairbanks to Anchorage gave us yet another up-close-and-personal look at this most amazing state. After we arrived in Anchorage we spent two nights in town and then camped out for 4 days near our worksite on the trail. Our job was to complete a boardwalk across a low-lying area, and I think we did a pretty good job for a bunch of non-construction folks! I like to think I've done my bit in helping future mushers get to Nome!

The Antarctic (Kayaking with Penguins)

IN THE SPRING OF 2016, I RECEIVED A NOTICE FROM ROAD Scholar describing a trip to the Antarctic. I had never planned to visit this distant outpost, mainly because it was so expensive ($10-15,000). These Road Scholar folks are clever, though. They offered an early-bird special for only $7,999 (including a private cabin on the ship). This was March, and the trip wasn't until December. A confirmed bargain hunter—I was hooked! Another major deciding factor was that I would be there on my birthday (81st), December 21. Instead of celebrating on the shortest day of the year it would be the longest in the Southern Hemisphere. Once again, how could I resist!

Leaving Eugene, I flew to Dallas and then on to Santiago, Chile. Arriving the next morning, somewhat zombie-like, I met the rest of the group and we were driven through rush-hour traffic to our hotel. When I left Eugene it was in the middle of winter (mid-30s to 40s). In Santiago, it was the middle of summer, so after stashing my bags I went out by the pool to crash. That afternoon, somewhat restored, we were taken on a city bus tour of Santiago. It seemed a very attractive place as we motored through town—a mix of modern and old structures. Santiago used to be a major shipping port, but after the Panama Canal was completed it lost the major portion of its trade. That evening we had an early dinner in the hotel and then to bed. Our departure the next morning was at 4:30 to enable us to catch the 3-hour flight to Punta Arenas at the southerly tip of South America. Here, our Norwegian ship, the *Midnatsol* (*Midnight Sun*) awaited us. It held some 300 passengers, and our group of about 50 fit right in. My cabin was super—not as small as I had expected. It had a large window providing a lovely outlook, two beds, a desk and a chair (for journal writing) plus a private bath. Since I was alone I could use the other bed for a couch. It also had a TV which I didn't use. The Road Scholar group had our special area in the dining room so we could keep in touch with one another easily. And the food—oh my! As I have stated previously, I am definitely not a foodie, so the multiple offerings at each meal were almost overwhelming. Being that the *Midnatsol* was a Norwegian ship, there were fish offerings at every meal, including breakfast. I did not crave smoked herring at 8 a.m. and much preferred my bacon/ham and eggs, along with a delicious variety of breads, in the morning. I was a bit more adventurous at the other meals. Breakfast and lunch were served buffet style, while dinner was a sit-down affair. Fortunately, the ship was very casual—no dress codes.

When we first boarded, we were given a credit card with which to make purchases during the voyage. This covered gift shop items. booze and any extra activities (like kayaking) we might choose to take part in. We were also given a terrific-looking hooded rain jacket to be worn when we left the ship and took junkets in zodiaks. These rubber, raft-like vessels, which held about 12 people, carried us almost daily to a landing on shore where we could explore more intimately the terrain we were sailing by. Sometimes we would take hikes (one day we climbed up a caldera) and sometimes we would just stroll around with the penguins. These very appealing birds have no predators on land and, consequently, are not at all fearful of humans. In fact, we were told to get no closer than 10 feet so as not to make them feel we were invading their space. Penguins live 3/4 of their lives in the ocean and come ashore only to breed in the summer (hence the timing of our trip). They nest in piles of rocks since no vegetation is available. This seems to work out just fine. It was such a joy to see the penguins waddle- around. One of my shipmates wryly exclaimed, "You'd waddle, too, if you had no ankles!" One of the more amusing things they seemed to enjoy doing was to sit on their butts and slide down hills. They've apparently learned how to conserve energy!

Early on, not long after leaving Punta Arenas, one of the high-lights of the trip was to dock at Cape Horn and climb up to the lighthouse. The sea in this area is often so rough that landing here is not possible. We definitely lucked out—a calm sea and a bright sunny day. Nearing the top of a long wooden stairway the old lighthouse came into view. As I stood there and gazed out I thought of all the navigators of yore who had braved this treacherous spot to get to the new world. From Cape Horn we headed south towards the Antarctic Peninsula through what is now known as the Drake Passage. On our passage, however, it was so smooth that the captain drubbed it Drake Lake. I had brought along Dramamine, but never had to use it.

Another of our memorable outings was a bit of snowshoeing. I signed up thinking it would be flat—not. Our guide proceeded to lead us up a fairly steep hill which eventually led to a view—great outlook, but tough getting there. The uphill didn't bother me so much, but old knees don't much like downhills. Once back on the ship I headed directly to the outdoor hot tub on deck and enjoyed a glass of wine while blissfully soaking away any aches in the steamy water. Probably the most unexpected outing of the trip was the opportunity to go kayaking. Yes, kayaking in Antarctica—who woulda thunk? I am a decent flat-water kayaker in my home state of Oregon (with its many lovely lakes) so I wasn't fearful, just curious as to what it would be like in this very different environment. What was decidedly different was the scenery. No Doug firs towering above the shoreline (or vegetation of any kind for that matter). Instead, we paddled past seals lounging on ice floes (who calmly ignored us) and gazed into icy crevasses whose interiors gave off an unearthly azure glow. To get outfitted for this event, in the interests of safety, took almost an hour. The organizers didn't want to lose anyone to hypothermia in the event of an unexpected dip in icy waters. Those of us who chose to partake in this activity were instructed to meet in a room clad only in our long johns and socks. There, we were incredibly layered up. The last layer being a wet suit which I could hardly get my head through it fit so snugly. Once out on the water, however, it was definitely worth the tedious preparation. I had never paddled in a two-person kayak before and was put in the front seat. At first I tried to steer the boat but was soon told by my "ship mate" that this is done by the person in back who controls the rudder—live and learn!

There are no towns in Antarctica, only research stations—home to a dozen or so countries. One day we moored off Port Lockroy, a tiny British station, where some of the inhabitants came on board selling postcards and stamps (as well as a few souvenir items). As an avid postcard sender I bought a bunch and then spent the afternoon writing them on the deck of our ship while gazing out intermittently at the incredible Antarctic scenery—snow-capped mountains simply rise up out of the sea! In all my travels, I have rarely seen scenery quite so stunning.

In addition to the activities off the ship, there were also excellent programs on board. Each evening we watched a video showing us what was on tap for the next day. There were also presentations giving us historical information about the region, as well as flora and fauna info. One evening/morning in the middle of the night, the loudspeaker in my cabin came to life announcing that there was a pod of whales alongside the ship. Quickly pulling on rain pants and parka over my PJ's, I hurried out on deck to see this spectacle. It was almost unworldly to see these huge creatures cavorting in the moonlight!

A fitting finish to this adventure was the captain's farewell dinner which included numerous champagne toasts. The following morning, December 21, I was treated to a rousing rendition of "Happy Birthday" at breakfast before leaving the ship.

— CHAPTER 21 —

ADDITIONAL NORTH AMERICAN ADVENTURES

Backpacking on Wheels

IN 2015 I TRIED SOMETHING A LITTLE DIFFERENT WHICH I called "backpacking on wheels." With my love for both back-packing and long drives I decided to combine the two. I out-fitted my little Honda Fit with a very comfortable foam rubber mattress, a sleeping bag, my butane backpacker's stove, a pan, a cup, a knife, a spork and two gallons of water. To this I added instant oatmeal, ramen noodles, some instant dinners, crackers, peanut butter, processed cheese beef jerky, coffee and—what I definitely don't take when I'm backpacking—a jug of wine. Once loaded up, I headed for Burlington, Vermont—home of my friend Fran. In this month-long odyssey I ate at restaurants only half-a dozen times (not counting "senior coffee" breaks at McDonalds) and only splurged on a motel every fourth night— to clean up and check my e-mail. This proved to be a very workable plan, saving me considerable bucks. Many of my "car camps" were free. Pull-offs in the woods were great when I was away from civilization. My favorite sign in a city was the big "H" indicating a hospital nearby. To me it meant "hotel." There are always people coming and going at hospitals, and no one paid any attention to me—even when I raised my hatchback in the parking lot and prepared meals. And, of course, the proximity of a restroom was also a plus.

I began my journey with a kayak on my roof rack and a National Parks "Senior Pass" in my glove compartment. This pass is available to anyone 62+ and grants free entry to all national parks as well as half-price in all federal campgrounds. At a one-time cost of only $10.00 it is absolutely the best bargain for an active senior. It has now gone up to $80.00 but is still an great bargain. My plan was to visit as many national park/monuments along the way as I could.

From Eugene I headed to central Oregon to visit friends in Sunriver and then turned north towards Montana and Glacier National Park. The "Going to the Sun" road through the park was truly awesome, and a paddle on McDonald Lake was lovely with views of the surrounding peaks. Continuing east to North Dakota I tried to find Theodore Roosevelt National Park, but major summer road repair detours took me well off course and I never did find it. Next was Voyageurs National Park on the U.S.-Canadian border. I hadn't realized this was a "no-roads" park (entry by boat only) so continued my drive through International Falls into Canada. After going through customs and changing some money, I soon found myself driving along the beautiful north shore of Lake Superior. Then on through Ontario and into Quebec. I eventually reached the outskirts of Montreal where I needed to turn south to Burlington. I figured the 50-mile drive would be a cinch—not! There are so many roads going in and out of Montreal that it was extremely difficult to figure out which one I needed to follow. After almost an hour of driving aimlessly in the suburbs I finally managed to make my way across the border,

The visit with Fran was wonderful. We had met in Eugene about 25 years earlier in the kayak world. I had just moved up from L.A and soon got in with a group of kayaking women. This was an activity I had never done in California, and I found it to be great fun. I soon had a kayak of my own. One of the adventures our little group undertook was to paddle up the Willamette River from Eugene to Corvallis (about 35 miles). We took three days, camping overnight on little islands in the river. Having moved to Burlington,

Fran's local waterway is now Lake Champlain, bordering Vermont and upstate New York. Here, we had a delightful paddle and stayed overnight at a little cabin she owns by the lake

Continuing my journey south, after a delicious stop at Ben and Jerry's, I took a short hike on the Appalachian Trail. I definitely wanted to set foot on this famous trail after having completed the Pacific Crest Trail. I found it to be much rockier and "rootier" than the PCT. From there I continued south and paid a visit to Val-Kill in Hyde Park, New York. This was Eleanor Roosevelt's very own special domain where she lived with two dear friends. It is now a National Monument. From time to time Eleanor entertained various world leaders of the day in this modest abode, and it was most interesting to reflect upon this when walking in their footsteps. But what I enjoyed most was walking directly in Eleanor's footsteps on the mile-long path surrounding her home—now dubbed "Eleanor's Walk." She was said to have taken this stroll almost daily (sometimes twice a day). I then headed further south to the Delaware Water Gap. This is a national recreation area along the Delaware River (yes, the one that George Washington crossed!). I was very glad to be camping along its banks in the summertime. One of my favorite "happy hours" of the trip was sitting in my beach chair and watching the sun go down over this beautiful, tranquil river.

Now it was time to head back west. My next stop was the only National Park in Ohio—Cuyahoga Valley NP. Its claim to fame being that it is situated along the Erie and Ohio Canal towpaths. The visitors' center was closed when I arrived, so I just parked in their parking lot for the night. The next morning I had a wonderful stroll along this historic path. These canals were the lifeblood of commerce during the late 1800s. Remnants of original construction are still visible. Then on through Indiana and a hellish drive along the outskirts of Chicago during morning rush hour. Nothing like having cars on either side of you whizzing at 70+ miles an hour and trying to stay in your lane when you're not exactly sure which lane you should be in!

From here, through the mid-west, the traffic eased up considerably. I wasn't always sure what lane to be in, but at least I had a minute or two to decide. Took a turn through Des Moines and had a look at the city's beautiful gold-domed capitol building. Then on to North Platte, Nebraska. Why North Platte? Because I had found on the internet a 5K to run there. I was definitely having running-withdrawal anxiety from my lack of races on this trip, but thanks to the "Running in the USA" website I found this event. The folks putting on the event seemed just as excited as I was to be there. They had never had a runner from Oregon before. I even got interviewed by the local TV station. And to top it off, I won an "Oscar." The race was for the benefit of restoring a roaring twenties theater and had a Hollywood theme. Age-division winners were presented with an Oscar which now sits proudly on my piano

Next came the mountainous gem of Rocky Mountain National Park in Colorado. The night before navigating the incredibly-engineered serpentine road through the park was spent in the parking lot of the Estes Park Hospital. I got a little musical accompaniment that evening as a group of local musicians was performing at the entrance to the hospital. Free accommodation and a free concert—such a deal! The next day, after taking in the marvels of the park, I found myself at a campground at its base on the other side. I had read that a section of the Continental Divide Trail came through this very spot. After all, I had already hiked a bit of the Appalachian Trail and now wanted add a taste of the CDT to my repertoire on this trip (I had previously done a small section in New Mexico with another avid septuagenarian backpacker, Mary, a lay preacher whose trail name is Medicare Pastor.) The three national long-distance trails in the United States are the Pacific Crest Trail, the Appalachian Trial and the Continental Divide Trail. I have now set foot on them all.

My final national park was Dinosaur, on the Colorado-Utah border. This had to be my favorite due to the "wow" factor of its inhabitants. Visitors overlook a wall imbedded with bones that are millions of years old. And children (or anyone for that matter) are encouraged to touch them—what an amazing hands-on experience. So different from looking up something on Google! One exhibit, however, was under glass and not touchable. It was the huge, very intact skull of a beast somewhere around 150 million years old— absolutely incredible!

From Dinosaur, I continued west through Nevada on U.S. Route 50—so-called "America's Loneliest Road"—which actually has some stunning high desert and mountainous landscapes. Then past Reno and into California through Lake Tahoe. I was looking forward to putting my kayak into that gorgeous lake. After paddling for about half an hour, however, my enjoyment came to a sudden end when I was pulled over and cited by the lake police for not having a life jacket. I tried to talk my way out of it by pleading ignorance, but to no avail. That citation was one souvenir I could have done without, but all in all it was a small price to pay for a magnificent month on the road. Several days later, after stopping by to see old friends Pat and Roe in Santa Rosa, California, I returned home to the best place of all—Eugene, Oregon!

Dogsleding in the North Woods

IN FEBRUARY OF 2004, I HEADED TO NORTHERN MINNESOTA for an entirely new adventure—dogsleding. One doesn't do much of this growing up in L.A. The brochure from Elderhostel sounded most inviting—except for the weather. There were two sessions offered. It mentioned that their January session could encounter temps of down to minus-20. The February session, however was more likely to be between zero and thirty—almost tropical! I signed up for February. Again, Fran joined on this venture. She's always up for stuff like this.

As Fran has an old school friend who now lives in Minneapolis, we joined forces in that city and stayed at her home before our mushing. She was a delightful hostess and even offered to drive us up to the camp—some five hours north of Minneapolis. This was a real coup, as we hadn't known just how we would get there—not really wanting to rent a car in the unfamiliar wintry conditions.

We were quartered at a YMCA camp about 100 miles south of the Canadian border. The cabins were heated and had toilets. The shower house was down a path, but reasonably convenient. Actually, I used it only once because the water was not very hot. I preferred to wash up in the basin in our bathroom where the water *was* hot. The dining hall was almost 1/4 mile from the cabin, but it was a lovely walk on a snowy path through a forest.

As I stated earlier, the focus of this trip was dogsleding, but we also got in some snowshoeing and X/C skiing. On the "doggie" days" we'd go out for a couple of hours, stop for lunch along the trail, and then mush back. The dogs were fabulous! They arrived in a van which contained a double layer of doggie boxes (two per box). Before they are taken out of their boxes, all is quiet. But as soon as we began harnessing them and attaching their leads (yes, we did this ourselves), the cacophony started. The dogs live to pull sleds, and they simply can't wait to get going! These are not the big Siberian husky/malamutes one expects but a much smaller breed called Alaskan Huskies (a somewhat-mixed breed). The females weigh in at just 30-35 pounds, with the males going up to 50 or so pounds. Small they may be, but all muscle! There were six dogs to each sled and two humans. One human stood at the back and drove while the other one sat in the sled (we took turns). The only instruction given to us was to point out the braking system. It consisted of a rubber pad between the two sled runners which you stood on to slow things down (standing on either one leg or two, depending on how quickly you wanted to slow down). There was also a metal bar on which you stomped if you wanted to come to a full stop. That was it. They said we'd soon get the hang of it. We did. Our teams took off at approximately 20-second intervals. Of course, I wanted to be the first one to drive and so experienced the initial jolt when the team was untied and we suddenly surged forward. Oh, I forgot one more instruction—the most important of all—DON'T EVER LET GO OF THE SLED (i.e. steering mechanism)! Well, this inadvertently happened to several of us, including me. At one point, when we were stopped briefly on the trail, I looked behind me to see what was going on. All of a sudden, not feeling any pressure of the reins, my team lurched forward causing my hands slip off the "handlebar"—OOPS! The dogs then surged forward and I tumbled off the sled (not hurt in the soft snow). They were MADLY trying to catch up with the team in front of us while I ran behind them trying to get them to stop. This was the wrong order of things! Fortunately, our leader soon came to the rescue—first checking that I was all right and then untangling the dogs and their harnesses. Shame-facedly, I then got back on the sled and hung on with a death grip.

A more relaxing activity was experiencing a traditional Finnish sauna and then taking a dip in the lake (which was not nearly as relaxing!). The sauna was situated on the edge of a nearby lake. It was a large, rustic log building consisting of two rooms—a dressing room and the wood-fired sauna itself. The only illumination came from kerosene lamps which cast a very dim glow. This made it very difficult to recognize our fellow campmates except for those who happened to be sitting right next to us. Since we were all naked (men and women at separate times fortunately) and just beginning to get to know one another, the dim lighting was probably a good thing. After steaming in the 180-degree heat for about 15 minutes the idea was to run outside to the lake, with only a towel, and jump into a hole cut in the ice. I had heard of people doing this but never I thought I would be one of them. But what the heck, most of the others were game and I definitely wanted bragging rights. Oh, I mentioned we were naked—not quite. We were told to wear wool socks so as not to slip on the ice as we ran down the 30-foot or so trail from the sauna to the ice hole. Once there I sat briefly on the side getting up the nerve, then closed my eyes and dropped a short distance into the water. OMG—I have never felt anything so cold in my life! After my micro-second dip I shot up the small ladder on the opposite side of the hole in record time and ran back to the sauna (before my socks could freeze!). A couple of crazy ladies went for a double dip. Others, like myself, did leave the sauna a second time but only to engage briefly in a little (very little) bare-assed interpretive dancing under the moon—while giving our best imitation wolf calls. I'm quite sure that if any of these wild creatures had been within earshot they would have howled with amusement. I don't ever plan on repeating this experience!

Epilogue

The end of this book in no way indicates the end of my adventures. With the gift of continued good health and vigor, I'm looking forward to many more before I leave this earthly realm. The map in my garage still way too many places not yet marked with a stick pin. And when I do leave these earthly constraints, who knows where I'll soar? That will be the biggest adventure of all!

If you would like to be updated, my email address is
runkitty35@pacinfo.com

Made in the USA
San Bernardino, CA
06 July 2020